ANTHROPOLOGICAL PAPERS

MUSEUM OF ANTHROPOLOGY, UNIVERSITY OF MICHIGAN
NO. 62

THE DEMOGRAPHY OF THE SEMAI SENOI

BY
ALAN G. FIX

ANN ARBOR, MICHIGAN
1977

© 1977 Regents of The Univeristy of Michigan
The Museum of Anthropology
All rights reserved

Printed in the
United States of America

TABLE OF CONTENTS

I. INTRODUCTION	1
II. SEMAI SOCIO-GEOGRAPHICAL GROUPINGS	7
The Semai People	7
Supra-settlement Groupings	11
Settlements and Hamlets	13
III. MARRIAGE PATTERNS	21
Marriage Types	21
Termination of Marriage	28
Consanguineous Marriage and Inbreeding	30
IV. SEMAI AGE AND SEX STRUCTURE	37
V. DEMOGRAPHY OF THE SA AREA	47
Fertility	47
Mortality	55
Causes of Death	60
Migration	63
Population Growth	68
VI. LIFE TABLES AND STABLE POPULATION MODELS	71
VII. SIMULATION	91
The Program	92
Simulation Results	97
Variation in Vital Rates	103
VIII. CONCLUSIONS	113
BIBLIOGRAPHY	119

LIST OF TABLES

2.1	Distribution of population by Hamlet—SA Settlement.	19
3.1	Marital Status—Living Population	27
3.2	Marital Status—Living Population of SA Settlements	27
3.3	Number of Productive Matings.	29
3.4	Genealogical Information Available for Mated Pairs.	31
3.5	Frequency of Consanguineous Matings	32
3.6	Ratios of Opposite-Sexed First to Second Cousins	33
3.7	Frequency of Consanguineous Matings	34
4.1	Total Numbers of Aborigines Enumerated in the National Census of Malaya, 1911-1947.	38
4.2	Age-Sex Distributions, 1965 Census	42
4.3	Distribution of Population within the SA Area by Settlement.	45
4.4	Comparison of Age Composition of the Censuses	46
5.1	Sterility in Semai Women greater than 20 Years of Age.	50
5.2	Age-Specific Fertility Rates.	51
5.3	Average Number of Children Born to Living Women.	52
5.4	Age-Class Fertility Coefficients	52
5.5	Completed Family Sizes	53
5.6	Surviving Offspring of Women of Completed Fertility	56
5.7	Mortality Estimates—Brass Method	56
5.8	Infant Death Rates.	57
5.9	Age Specific Death Rates	58
5.10	Abridged Semai Life Table	59
5.11	Causes of Death—All Settlements—1950-1969	60
5.12	Migration, SA Settlement, 1960-1969	65
5.13	Birthplaces of the SA Area Population	66
5.14	Birthplaces of Married Pairs	66
5.15	Parent-Offspring Birthplaces	67
5.16	Annual Rates of Growth	69
6.1	East Semai Female Model Life Table.	79
6.2	East Semai Male Model Tife Table	81
6.3	Comparison of Model and Observed Age-Specific Fertility Rates.	81
6.4	Comparison of Model and Observed Sex Ratios	84
6.5	Comparison of Semai Model Rates to other Populations (Female).	88
7.1	Simulation Input	94
7.2	Simulation Output.	94

7.3	Comparison of Model and Cumulative Artificial Population Composition	100
7.4	Comparison of Crude Vital Rates of Model and Artifical Populations	102
7.5	Variation in Basic Demographic Parameters for Five Randomly Selected Artificial Populations	110

LIST OF FIGURES

2.1 Map showing the distribution of settlements in the study area 14
2.2 Sketch map of SA settlement 17
3.1 Age differences between spouses, total distribution 24
3.2 Age differences between spouses, partitioned distribution......... 25
4.1 Population pyramid, West Semai, 1965 Jabatan Orang Asli census... 40
4.2 Population Pyramid, East Semai, 1965 Jabatan Orang Asli census ... 41
4.3 Population Pyramid, SA area, SA settlement 45
6.1 Comparison of female cumulative age distribution (c_x) of the 1965 Pahang census (unsmoothed) with Cole and Demeny (1966) model distributing having $e_0 = 40$ and $r = 0.020$. 74
6.2 Comparison of female cumulative age distribution (c_x) with the best fitting model distribution from Weiss (1973) 78
6.3 Comparison of male cumulative age distrivtuion (c_x) with best fitting model distribution from Weiss (1973).................... 80
6.4 Comparison of empirical and model mortality rates 82
6.5 Graph of the sex ratio of the 1965 Pahang census by cumulative age. 85
7.1 Simplified flow chart of the simulation program............... 93
7.2 Deviation of the male artificial population composition for two runs.105
7.3 Distribution of crude rates for all runs 107
7.4 Variation of crude rates through time...................... 107
7.5 Distribution of annual growth rates based on ten-year intervals for four 200-year runs................................. 108

PREFACE

During 1968-69 I carried out an anthropological and genetic study among the Semai Senoi of Malaysia. The goals of this research were to identify the local breeding populations, measure the amount of genetic exchange between them and document the genetic effects of Semai population structure. These aims required the collection of an extensive body of demographic materials as well as cultural and genetic data. The results of the study were presented in my doctoral dissertation (Fix 1971) and in various subsequent publications. The present work constitutes a revision of portions of my dissertation supplemented by data from the 1965 census of aborigines which has been given a much expanded analysis.

Several individuals and institutions have provided me with guidance and assistance. My dissertation chairman Frank B. Livingstone, Department of Anthropology, University of Michigan, along with the other members of my committee, encouraged me and gave their helpful criticism during the dissertation work. Robert K. Dentan made many useful suggestions regarding field work with the Semai. I continue to lean heavily on his insightful analysis of Semai society (Dentan 1968). In Malaysia, the Department of Aboriginal Affairs (Jabatan Orang Asli) was very helpful. Frederick Dunn of the International Center for Medical Research, University of California, San Francisco gave encouragement, help, and much good counsel about the Orang Asli and Malaysia in general. Dr. J. M. Bolton, former medical officer for the Orang Asli, also made helpful suggestions and comments regarding suitable research sites and Semai health. I give many thanks to all.

Financial support for the field work came from National Institute of Mental Health Predoctoral Fellowship 2F1MH34,135 and attached grant 1T01MH11415. Additional support was provided by the University of California International Center for

Medical Research and Training through research grant A1 10051 to the Department of International Health, School of Medicine, University of California, San Francisco, from the National Institute of Allergy and Infectious Diseases, National Institutes of Health, U.S. Public Health Service. Funds for research assistants were provided by the Intramural Research Fund of the Academic Senate, University of California, Riverside. Computer time was provided by the Computer Allocation Committee, also of the University of Calfornia, Riverside.

Finally, and perhaps most importantly, thanks to my wife, Betsy Dickinson Fix, who helped at every stage of the research (especially with the computer programming) and to the Semai without whose cooperation nothing would have been accomplished.

CHAPTER I

INTRODUCTION

Interest in the demography of technologically "primitive" populations has a long history (Carr-Saunders 1922, Krzywicki 1934). In recent years this interest has continued and strengthened. In cultural anthropology, a concern with environmental factors and human adaptation has led naturally to a recognition of the importance of demography. Archaeologists have also incorporated population parameters into their models for much the same reasons. Even some demographers have become involved with small-scale populations. One such individual has concisely stated what are perhaps the two basic questions facing anthropological demographers (Howell 1973). These are: 1) "What levels and patterns of mortality and what levels and patterns of fertility have formed this population and maintained it in the long run?" 2) "How is the population pattern both a cause and an effect of the overall organization of [the group's] life?"

The first is a traditional demographic question. The second brings population properties into the mainstream of anthropological inquiry. Demography may need to be considered an element in the constellation of factors including environment and culture contact, among others, which interact to produce cultural patterns and human adaptation.

Along with the rising interest in demography among cultural and archaeological anthropologists, physical anthropologists and geneticists have also begun to appreciate the need to incorporate population data into their formulations (Cavalli-Sforza and Bodmer 1971). For example, Neel and his colleagues have repeatedly stressed (Neel 1970, Neel and Weiss 1975) that in order to understand the conditions under which most of human biological evolution occurred, the population structure of living groups practicing hunting and gathering and/or simple agriculture must be studied.

Despite these several foci of interest in the demography of technologically "primitive" or "anthropological" populations, some investigators continue to state that little detailed data exist for comparative purposes (Neel and Weiss 1975).

Although this may be an extreme view, it is not difficult to imagine why anthropological demography is not highly developed. As Howell (1973) notes, anthropological populations are the most difficult to study demographically due to their small size and to the lack of records of vital events. Traditionally, demographers have dealt with large national populations for which relatively accurate censuses and vital registries exist. Few anthropologists can hope for these kinds of data. Given their other concerns, anthropologists have tended not to expend the enormous effort necessary to amass demographic information which would, in spite of their attempts, be considered very poor by demographer's standards.

However, in recent years, two techniques which promise to simplify the analysis of small scale populations have come increasingly into use: stable population analysis and computer simulation. Both have been used by anthropologists to arrive at a better understanding of the demography of anthropological populations (Weiss 1973, MacCluer et al. 1971).

Providing that certain assumptions are met, stable population methods allow an internally consistent picture of the demography of a group to be gained from relatively scanty data (U.N. 1967). The basic assumptions are that the fertility and mortality schedules of the population being investigated fall within the range of the model tables employed, and that these schedules have not undergone systematic large-scale changes within the preceeding 100 years (Howell 1973). Although it may be difficult to be certain that the second of these assumptions is justified in many anthropological populations, the problem is no more difficult than that confronting demographers applying these methods to developing countries (Brass et al. 1968).

Similarly, Monte Carlo simulation techniques may be used to gauge the internal consistency of demographic parameters and to explore the long-range implications of demographic processes in small populations (Dyke and MacCluer 1974).

In the present work, these techniques will be applied to an extensive body of data from the Semai Senoi, a swidden farming group of Malaysia. The basic goal is to answer Howell's first question; i.e., what are the patterns of mortality and fertility characterizing the Semai population. At the same time the comparison of empirical estimates of vital rates, stable models and simulation may also contribute to the methodology of analyzing small populations particularly with respect to the degree of variability in rates to be expected between sub-populations in space and within populations through time.

As Dentan (1968) has stressed, the Semai do not form a "tribe" in the sense that they are united in a single political entity. At the same time, all Semai share dialects of a common language and a common belief system, and are geographically contiguous. For some purposes the Semai "people" might be considered as a unit. In the present work, it is necessary to distinguish between more acculturated and less acculturated Semai, since contact with other cultures has had an impact on the characteristics of the population. It is probably impossible to reconstruct the pristine demographic Eden of the Semai; nonetheless, the aim of this work is to describe the characteristics of a relatively unaffected division of the total population. It is to be hoped that this description will provide suitable comparative material for other anthropological demographers.

The analysis of this population has been considerably strengthened by the availability of a census of the whole population. The Malaysian Department of Aboriginal Affairs kindly provided me with their 1965 census of over 12,000 Semai. Of these, more than 3800 individuals occupy relatively unacculturated areas. Although, as will be seen in chapter 4, this census was not totally accurate particularly with respect to the aging of individuals, the large number of persons counted within it provides a base for the application of stable population methods. Certainly the census size exceeds that normally available to the anthropological demographer based on his or her independent effort.

Other attributes of Semai demographic structure were obtained by the author within one region of the Semai distribution. The limitation of these data include the typical problems of small base population, questionable representativeness, and uncertain accuracy. In combination with the population composition from the 1965 census, however, it was possible to achieve a reasonably good fit to a stable population model (chapter 6). In addition to the empirically-derived data, a description of the overall characteristics of the population which is internally consistent and matches the empirical in a variety of respects is thus available for comparative purposes.

Finally, the stable population model characteristics have been incorporated in a stochastic computer simulation (chapter 7). The mean demographic parameters of the artificial populations generated in the simulation closely match the stable model for a variety of measures. However, over the short term, the simulated population characteristics fluctuate rather markedly. This is the sort of variation from year to year and decade to decade that one might expect to find in small anthropological populations. The degree of variation seen in the simulated populations allows a baseline estimate of that encountered by the fieldworker gathering demographic data over a short time span. It is a technique which might be used to gauge how close the empirical field data might be to the underlying "true" rates operating in the long run. Moreover, such estimates of variation provide a picture of the amount of variation in complex demographic rates and ratios which are difficult to handle analytically.

Fieldwork

The data upon which this work is based were collected in Malaysia during a thirteen month period (April 1968 to May 1969). The bulk of this period was spent in seven settlements in a relatively unacculturated area of the Semai distribution. In all settlements, a household census and a sketch map were made. The census was used as the starting point for genealogies and reproductive histories. In the main study settlement, reproductive histories were obtained from all adults (or, in the case of recently deceased individuals, from spouses or close relatives). In the other settlements, the limited time available did not allow a complete and accurate enumeration of the living and dead offspring of all the adults to be performed. However, a relatively large sample was collected. Genealogies for the main study settlement were more complete. Since many individuals possessed a wide net of relatives in many settlements, however, it was often possible to have a good idea of the genealogies of persons in other settlements before visiting them. Details could be supplied within the already established framework. In this way, a set of genealogies representing the ancestry of most of the population of the study area was constructed. It should be pointed out, however, that information regarding the generations preceding the oldest living individuals is sketchy. The method used in the construction of these genealogies allows multiple checks on informants' statements so that what is available seems reasonably accurate, but many pedigrees are not particularly deep.

Information on each individual, living or dead, was compiled on a set of data sheets which were constantly updated throughout the course of the research. For individuals who appeared only in genealogies, this information was solicited from a variety of informants and was thus amenable to checking. The completeness and accuracy of this information varied between individuals. In general, the data on long-dead individuals are lacking or of dubious quality. Information concerning those more recently deceased or currently living are, correspondingly, more complete.

During the gathering of these data, other aspects of Semai culture were simultaneously observed in day-to-day interaction. Many informants were questioned about various matters such as the histories of settlements and their beliefs and attitudes. In addition, census and other materials were made available to me through the kindness of the Malaysian Department of Aboriginal Affairs (Jabatan Orang Asli) and the Gombak Aborigine Hospital.

CHAPTER II

SEMAI SOCIO–GEOGRAPHICAL GROUPINGS

The Semai People

The Semai are the numerically largest group of the several aboriginal (Orang Asli) populations of the Malayan Peninsula (see Dentan 1968, frontispiece). Their present distribution is along the flanks of the Main Range, the mountainous backbone of the peninsula. Numbering approximately 12,750, they live principally in the states of Perak and Pahang.

The Semai may best be regarded as the "aggregate of people who speak dialects of the Semai language" (Dentan 1968). They do not form a political unit at the tribal level. Indeed, the dialect variation is great enough that Semai speakers from widely separated areas may have some difficulty in communicating.[1] Nonetheless, there is a general sense of identity implied in the term.[2]

Linguistically, Semai is included in the Austroasiatic family and is thus related to languages spreading across Southeast Asia from Assam and Burma to Cambodia and Vietnam (Lebar et al. 1964). Benjamin (1973) has classified Semai (along with several other aboriginal languages of Malaya, Temiar, Mah Meri, Semelai, Che Wong, and various Negrito groups) in the Aslian (or Senoi) group of Austroasiatic (Mon-Khmer). Although Semai may definitely be a member of Mon-Khmer, it does appear that the relationship is somewhat distant (Dentan 1968) which implies a long separate history for the Aslian speakers. Presently, they exist

---

[1]This was certainly my experience traveling in different areas. See also Diffloth (1968).

[2]See Benjamin's (1966a) excellent discussion of this subject in reference to the closely related Temiar.

as an enclave within the larger Malay linguistic area, a family unrelated to Austroasiatic.

Archaeological evidence for Semai origins is not extensive. The linguistic connection with northern Southeast Asia would suggest a derivation from that area or, perhaps, from an ancient widespread Austroasiatic group including the Malayan Peninsula within its boundaries. The widespread noninsular Asian Hoabhinian stone tool assemblage, which includes flaked core tools, utilized flakes, and grinding tools, is represented by several sites in Malaya (Dunn 1970) and persists until roughly the second millennium B.C. (Cant 1972). This is followed by a Neolithic occupation, evidenced by polished stone tools and pottery. A radiocarbon date of 4800 ± 800 B.P. has been obtained for a level marking the earliest Neolithic from latest Hoabhinian at a cave site in Pahang (Dunn 1966). Later materials representing a bronze and iron-using people have been ascribed to miners or traders entering the Peninsula (Cant 1972).

Some have suggested that the Semai are descendants of the Neolithic people of Malaya (Cant 1972). If so, they have discarded any archaeological attributes associated with that group, such as stone tools and pottery, in favor of iron trade tools and bamboo and rattan baskets (Dunn 1970).

But whatever their original homeland and whoever their ancestors might have been, they have apparently inhabited Malaya for a considerable number of centuries if not millenia. Their own traditions place the origin of all the aborigines in the western state of Perak at *Sakai Jadi* (literally, "become aborigine"). From there, all the present day aboriginal groups spread to their present territories, gradually lost their ancestral speech and adopted their present languages. However inadequate this tradition may be as history, it nonetheless provides an interesting folk account of a plausible colonization of the area by founding groups (Birdsell 1957).

In more recent times, the areal distribution of the Semai has shrunk, mainly as a result of the spread of the Malays. The early history of the Malays is almost as obscure as that of the Semai but it is established that by the twelfth century Sri Vijaya, an Indianized Buddhist empire based on Sumatra was extending control to the mainland. Even in the interior, groups of Malays were already mining gold by the fourteenth century (Cant 1972). From this time to the present Malay and later Chinese immigrants have continued to encroach upon what had once been Semai territory. Thus, it is most likely that in the past, the Semai occupied large portions of the Perak lowlands. Today, those Semai groups living in the lowlands are islands in a sea of technologically more dominant Malays. The Pahang Semai in the east have also been reduced in their territorial holdings. The important tin and gold fields of southwestern Pahang may well have once been Semai country but this area has been exploited by miners from very early times (Cant 1972).

Contact with Malays has not only resulted in territorial loss but has also introduced a variety of items which are now integral parts of Semai culture. Trade for iron tools, such as axe heads and machetes, certainly has been going on for generations; according to living Semai, they have "always" had iron tools. Most of the principal crops of the Semai are introduced. Manioc (a staple) and corn (a minor crop) are American in origin, as are many others. Even rice appears to be a late introduction, and some Semai are even now reported to depend on millet as their basic grain.

In addition to trade, slave raiding may also have been practiced over a long period and presumably did not end until early in the twentieth century (Dentan 1968).

Trading and raiding have undoubtedly had effects on the Semai, but the really profound changes in the Semai way of life are more recent. These changes have not uniformly affected all Semai. Indeed, the present cultural heterogeneity of Semai subgroups is mainly a function of differential contact with other Malaysian traditions, especially Malay, but in recent times Chinese as well. As might be expected, lowland groups have been influenced to a much greater degree by the culture of neighboring Malays than the more remote hill dwellers. Differences which might have arisen from environmental factors are masked by this effect since the gradient in altitude, the primary environmental parameter in the tropics, parallels the gradient in acculturation.

In one sense, however, the two factors, environment and contact, have worked in concert to affect Semai life patterns. The physical environment itself has been profoundly affected by Malay, Chinese, and European economic activities. Particularly with the onset of systematic large-scale mining of tin deposits in Perak from the 1850s on, vast portions of the lowlands have been transformed into wastelands of tin tailings. By the early 1900s, rubber cultivation began to replace the jungle in many areas not already made unsuitable for agriculture by mining. These activities severely restricted Semai opportunities for traditional swidden agriculture and associated hunting and gathering, a system which requires low population density and much land.

The most apparent effect, then, of these developments has been in technology and economy. In the Perak lowlands, many traditional Semai territories were expropriated for tin mines. In some cases the Semai themselves became small-scale miners. Noone (1939) describes a group with a small tin mine and a rubber plantation in the 1930s. By this period, these people were already living on purchased rice. Currently, several villages no longer have enough land remaining to practice swidden cultivation and depend almost entirely on cash received from rubber holdings for subsistence. The members of at least one lowland Semai village now practice wet rice agriculture. Another highland group is engaged in wage labor on a tea estate.

Not all changes in Semai technology and economy stem from the private sphere of the Malaysian economy. The Department of Aboriginal Affairs (Jabatan Orang Asli) has for many years been gradually introducing medical care, rubber and fruit tree cash crops, schools, and other services to the Semai (Baharon 1967, Carey 1973). A particularly important influence has been the establishment of a hospital for aborigines at Ulu Gombak, medical posts in many Semai settlements including some in remote highland communities, and the incorporation of young Semai as members of the medical service (Bolton 1968). The increase in health care has begun to have noticeable effects on the demography of the Semai as the incidence of diseases is reduced and individuals who would formerly have died now survive.

Changes are not confined to the economy, however; where Semai have been in close contact for many years with non-Semai, social organization and beliefs have also been affected. Dentan (1968) provides numerous examples of contrasts between the more acculturated Western and the less acculturated Eastern Semai.

The Semai tribe, then, is not a homogeneous unit. The economies of particular villages range from wage labor to traditional horticulture, supplemented by hunting and gathering. While retaining their common language and many cultural attributes, the Semai now represent a collection of sub-groups in various stages of transition toward an accomodation with the larger Malaysian society.

The phenomenon of fragmentation, however, is not a new development. Traditional Semai society was also a collection of politically autonomous communities. However, these communities were relatively undifferentiated; each community was culturally similar and functionally equivalent to all other communities. Thus, in spite of present day diversity, it is possible to describe the population characteristics of an array of the less influenced communities and, with some confidence, attempt to generalize about the traditional population.

Supra-settlement Groupings

The Semai social universe is not tightly organized into a series of hierarchical levels. As noted above, villages tend to be autonomous. Nonetheless, some groupings may be distinguished, although their boundaries are not always sharply drawn and the criteria defining them may overlap. One such group includes the settlements along a major river and its tributaries.

Throughout the hill regions of Semai territory, streams and rivers are the main arteries of travel. Dentan (1964) has argued that the contact between settlements occupying one river basin which results from the ease of travel within the basin fosters the development of a loosely defined grouping named for the principal river. The principle holds even in more acculturated areas where modern roads now seem to serve as rivers (Dentan 1965). Benjamin (1966b) describes an equivalent grouping for the closely related Temiar, pointing out that the Temiar total world view is markedly oriented toward the pattern of rivers. He also stresses the sense of community and ease of social relations among inhabitants of villages in one river system. This is particularly true in the middle reaches of the rivers where one valley is divided from another by high ridges.

The members of the river valley group seldom or never meet as a unit although Dentan (1968) points out that they cooperated in dealing with outsiders. During the Emergency[3] some upriver and

---

[3]Following World War II, the Malayan Communist party began a campaign to gain independence from the British. Since much of the military activity occured in the jungle, some groups of Semai were involuntarily affected. Groups in communist-held territory were expected to provide food and guide/porter services for the guerillas while those Semai in fringe jungle areas worked with the Government. This situation (termed the Emergency) continued until 1960 although the fighting decreased greatly after 1956 (Kennedy 1967).

downriver groups were under conflicting pressures from Communist and Government troops. Under these unusual circumstances, upriver groups in Communist territory cooperated with the communists and at the same time looked out for the interests of downriver groups who were working with the Government and vice-versa. According to Dentan, an arrangement had been worked out between the respective Semai groups such that Semai associated with the winning side (Government or Communist) would claim that the other Semai had been coerced and were really 'pro-government' or 'pro-communist' all the time.

It has also been suggested that the river valley group is relatively endogamous (Dentan 1964). Given that river valleys serve as major routes of travel, and that people tend to marry those they visit (Boyce et al. 1967), this is not unreasonable. However, as Benjamin (1966) and I (Fix 1974) have pointed out, this is only a tendency. Many marriages occur between occupants of different river valleys, sometimes over relatively great distances.

It is also possible to recognize larger groupings of settlements than those occupying major river valleys. The Semai do not formally conceptualize these as entities but rather feel a vague sense of community within several river systems. The prime referent of these units is shared dialect. Diffloth (1968) sees "extreme dialectical diversification with regular sound correspondences" often associated with a river valley community. The river valley as a channel for visiting and communication may help to define the linguistic community. As in the case of endogamy, however, this is not absolute. For example, in the area in which I was located, individuals had little contact with people living some fifteen miles north along another major river system. Nonetheless, they know that the dialect spoken there is nearly identical to their own. These groups are considered less "foreign" than those from Perak or other areas with whom communication would be more difficult.

A third level of settlement groupings which may be delineated is the "cluster" (Dentan 1965, 1971). The criterion which defines a cluster is frequency of interaction. Cluster "members do not have face-to-face contact with all other members but do interact far oftener with each other than with nonmembers" (Dentan 1965). Dentan feels that clusters were once relatively endogamous but a similar argument may apply here as in the case of river valleys. The cluster also serves as the last refuge when disasters such as widespread crop failure strike a settlement. There is a general notion of kinship ties and commonality between its members, whereas members of another cluster are truly strangers.

These, then, are the main supra-settlement Semai social groupings: the tribe (clearly distinguished from nonaborigines, less clearly from other aborigine tribes), the dialect group, the cluster, and the river valley group. Their principal importance to the present study is that they define patterns of migration and, insofar as they are relatively homogeneous groups within the larger Semai society, they differ in degree of contact and in demographic characteristics.

Settlements and Hamlets

As is true of other aspects of culture, Semai settlement patterns have been differentially influenced by Malay contact. Many villages in the acculturated West are almost indistinguishable from Malay villages. Houses with tin roofs are relatively permanent constructions made from planks and are closely spaced together. They are surrounded by long-persisting *kampong* fruit trees (coconut, areca nut, jack fruit, etc.) and stands of rubber trees.

Rather than describe the many current varieties of Semai settlements, I will confine the discussion to a group of relatively unacculturated settlements from the eastern portion of the Semai distribution, the SA area[4]. Dentan (1968) may be consulted for a description of other patterns as well as for a slightly different analysis of the settlement pattern.

Semai settlements in the SA area are not villages in the usual sense of the term. Rather they are a series of hamlets strung out along a river and its tributaries for as many as one or two miles. These linear aggregations of hamlets are in turn separated by larger distances, usually the equivalent of at least a two-hour walk. Figure 2.1 shows the distribution of settlements in the SA area and provides a scale of the distances separating them.

Often the hamlets are composed of small, two- to five-family groups of close relatives. The individuals may all occupy one house, forming what Dentan (1965) described as an "extended

---

[4] This includes the seven communities visited and censused in 1969. "SA" derives from an abbreviation of the name of the largest settlement; the other settlements (also abbreviated) are KE, RU, KL, BU, KA, and CH. The settlements range in size from 50 to 272 persons and are spread over an area of 120 square miles.

THE DEMOGRAPHY OF THE SEMAI SENOI

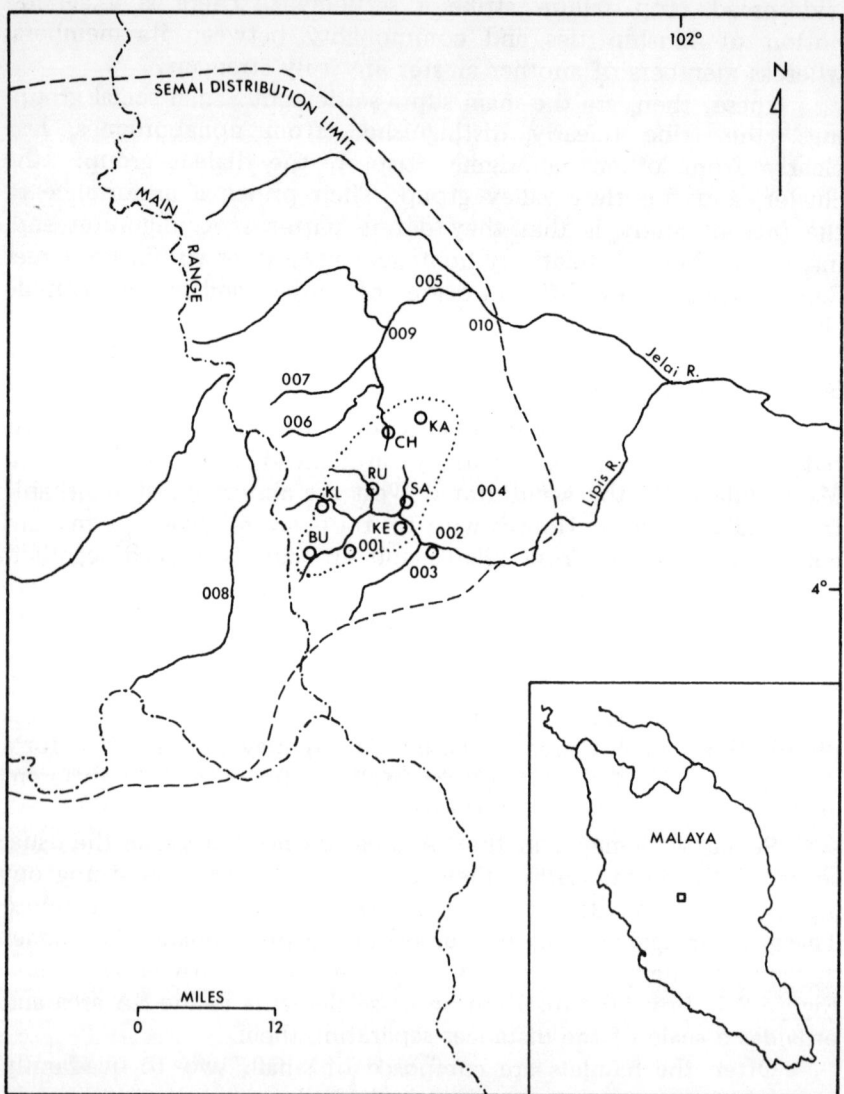

Fig. 2.1 Map showing the distribution of Semai settlements in the study area and their relationships to other settlements and tribes. Settlements are represented by circles; those inside the study area (enclosed by dotted line) are named; settlements which are outside the study area or abandoned are indicated by numbers. The dash-dotted line indicates state boundaries (which follow the Main Range from north to south). Reprinted by permission of publisher.

household", or several houses (Dentan's "homestead"). In the latter instance, one house is generally larger than the others and serves as the locus of communal activities.

Hamlets are not always composed of such small groups. There is a continuum in size from one-house, one-family hamlets to large communities containing as many as fifty individuals. Moreover, there is considerable variation in the dispersal of hamlets. As will be seen below, hamlets in SA settlement are within a fifteen-minute walk of each other. In other settlements, hamlets are more spread out. At CH, some are as much as an hour's walk from their nearest neighbor.

Hamlets usually take their names from a small stream nearby. Settlements may show a hierarchy of such names. Thus, for example, at SA settlement, everyone is a member of the SA group *(Mai SA)*. At the next lower level, two further distinctions are made between those living along the SA river proper and those on the RE river a little to the west; *Mai SA* and *Mai RE*. Within these two categories, other distinctions are made between groups living on tributaries of these rivers. Thus along the RE are found *Mai Cheba' Mehang, Mai Bareh Kemor*, etc. Furthermore, some family groups may be living near their fields at some distance from another hamlet. These will generally not be named localities but will be referred to as "the house of so-and-so" with or without the stream or hill name added. The hamlets are the main locus of personal interaction. Where hamlets are at some distance from each other, relations with other settlement members may be fairly infrequent. Even at SA, where hamlets are close together, most social life occurs within the hamlet.

Nonetheless, the residential unit which an SA area individual will name as his home in relation to other groups is the settlement. To a person from RU, all individuals living along the SA and RE rivers are Mai SA. Also when a Semai is asked where he lives by an outsider, the answer will refer to the settlement rather than the hamlet (see also Benjamin 1966b).

The settlement inhabitants' sense of community is also expressed in their joint headman. Although hamlets may have an older man who can act to mediate disputes, relations with *mai* or "outsiders" are handled by the settlement headman.

The settlement is thus an amalgam of hamlets which are the units of day-to-day interaction and communal activity, but is recognizable as a unit of closer solidarity than other groups of hamlets.

In some cases, hamlets may be short-term residence sites, as when a family or several families build a house near their fields. These sites are abandoned after the harvest of the rice crop. Other hamlet locations are of considerable antiquity. These sites are usually associated with long-bearing fruit trees, especially durian trees which may bear for several human generations. In fact, a common response to queries about the duration of occupation of a site includes the phrase "durian orchard of our great-grandfathers."

Several stands of old fruit trees are found within the area of a typical settlement. The fact that several of these sites are no longer occupied bears testimony to the impermanence of hamlet locations.

There are several reasons for this impermanence. The first of these is due to the nature of swidden or "shifting" horticulture. From year to year, fields are cut in new locales and the hamlet site is moved to provide easy access to the field. Secondly, the traditional response to a death in the hamlet was flight; houses were burned and new houses constructed some distance away.

Thus, over the short term, hamlet sites shift from spot to spot, usually within a small radius. Occasionally, however, sites may be abandoned entirely. Documentation of this process will be provided below.

The settlement, on the other hand, is generally a more permanent entity. It is territorially defined though its boundaries are not sharply demarcated. In the ethological sense, it might be regarded as a "home range" rather than a "territory," since the Semai do not defend their land against encroachment by outsiders. Warfare for territorial acquisition (like all forms of warfare) does not occur in Semai society. Land is not owned by individuals or corporate kin groups and is not considered a scarce good. Individuals or groups of individuals may enter a settlement area, take up residence and plant fields with no opposition by the resident group. After a suitable length of time, those people take on the name of the settlement in which they have established residence. Their ties with their former dwelling are not forgotten, but they have full rights to the use of land in the new settlement. Thus, for instance, several old men may make the observation that "all the old (by inference, true) members of that settlement are dead;

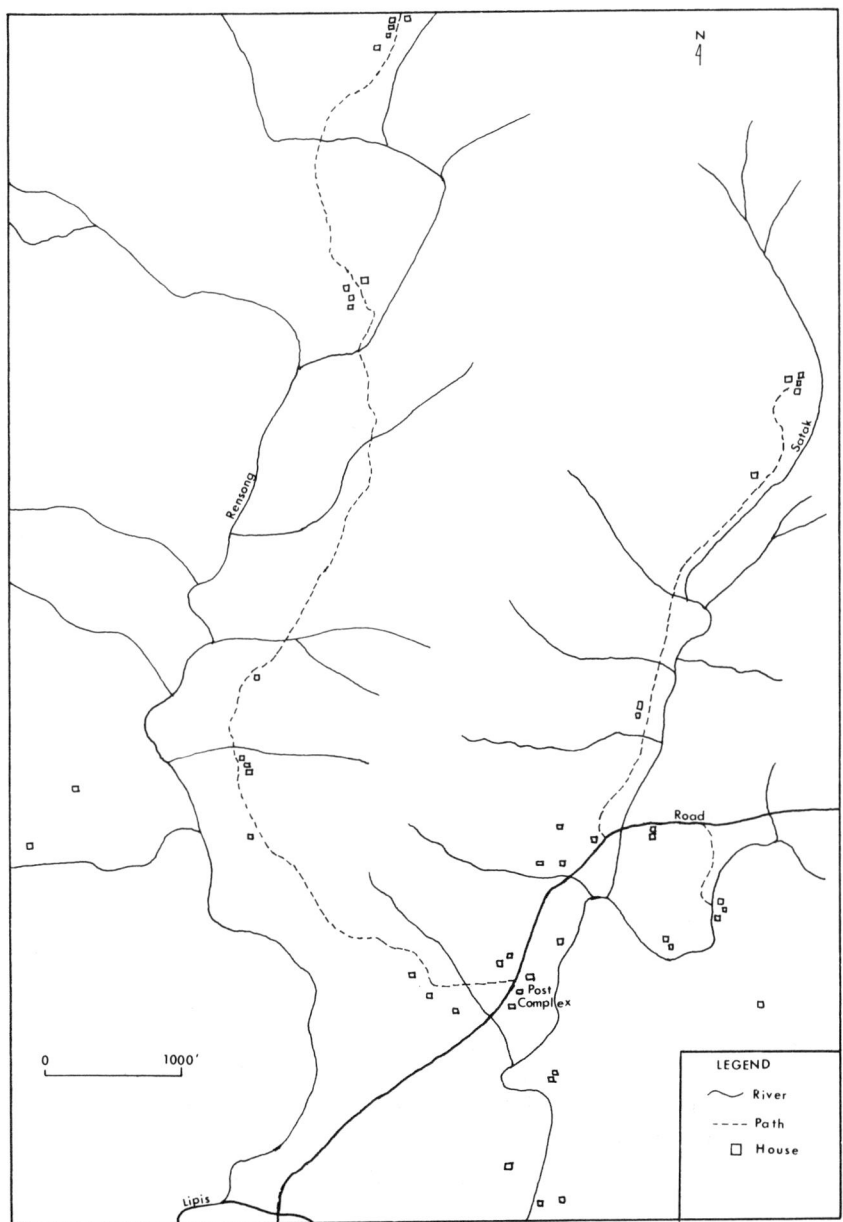

Fig. 2.2 Sketch map of SA settlement.

everybody living there now is from far away!" Nevertheless, most of the residents of that settlement may have been born there and consider themselves (and are considered by most members of other settlements) to be its true residents.

Over the long term then, the settlement as a social or kinship group changes. Some families leave less offspring than others; some groups move into the settlement from other areas. But the settlement as a focus of population concentration tends to persist.

This is not to say that settlement areas are never abandoned. In recent times Malay communities have been spreading and displacing some traditional Semai settlements and, in the past, epidemics have caused whole settlements to disperse. In general, however, the breaking up of a settlement occurs infrequently.

An explanation for the relative persistence of the settlement would undoubtedly include a number of factors, among them the fact that Semai population density is approximately at an equilibrium level below the point of total exploitation of all available land. This is a common situation among swidden cultivators (Carneiro 1960). At present, the Semai population in the SA area is not rapidly expanding (see chapter 5). Thus, demographic fluctuations can be adjusted by migration, and increases can be absorbed by the excess of land over and above what would be needed to support the mean population size within the settlement area.

The flexibility of Semai recruitment to a territory is such that the traditional division of the country into settlements can be maintained. Since the land bordering streams is preferred for horticulture, the river valleys tend to define the settlement area. The unoccupied land between settlement locales is exploited for game and jungle produce. Given the present population density, this land is not needed for agricultural exploitation.

In order to illustrate the lability of population composition of hamlets, the hamlets of SA settlement will be described for two dates, December 15, 1968, and April 15, 1969. Figure 2.2 shows the location of the hamlets in respect to each other and to the main topographic features of the area.

On the two dates, the distribution of population between the hamlets was as follows:

TABLE 2.1

DISTRIBUTION OF POPULATION
BY HAMLET—SA SETTLEMENT

House Group	December 15		April 15		Difference in No. Ind.
	Number of Houses	Number of Individuals	Number of Houses	Number of Individuals	
1	2	20	1	13	-7
2	7	36	6	31	-5
3	2	18	2	16	-2
4	3	13	4	19	+6
5	2	10	1	5	-5
6	2	12	2	18	+6
7	1	5	2	9	+4
8	6	30	2	14	-16
9	1	9	1	10	+1
10	3	17	4	22	+5
11	2	11	1	13	+2
12	3	11	2	11	0
13	3	12	2	7	-5
14	1	10	1	9	-1
15	3	14	3	14	0
16	4	20	3	20	0
17			1	5	+5
18	3	28	5	36	+8
19	1	2			-2
Total	49	278	43	272	-6

In the short span of four months, relatively large population rearrangements occurred. The changes came about as a result of the entrance of ten individuals into the settlement area, the departure of eighteen individuals (several of these people were visitors who spent approximately three weeks at SA), the birth of five children, and the death of two old women and one man. Furthermore, two marriages and three divorces resulted in the movement of individuals to different households. One house site near a field was abandoned when the couple living there left after the rice harvest in February. Another family set up a new household in order to be near a grove of rubber trees.

At SA most hamlet sites are within a fifteen-minute walk of each other and some are much closer. This is partially a recent trend stemming from new services being introduced by the Department of Aboriginal Affairs (JOA). A new school and medical post were built in 1963. In addition, a timber cutting operation was begun by a Chinese firm. In 1968, the company opened a road which passes through the SA settlement and continued several miles up the major river, of which the SA is a tributary, to the location of their operations. In order to take advantage of the facilities at the post, many households have moved within the last six years or so to their present location. This is particularly true of house groups one and two which are now located on the road. Several years ago, this group was living some distance up river, at a site which is now uninhabited.

The tendency as seen at SA settlement is, then, toward a coalescing of residential groups and a blurring of the spatial distinction between hamlets which results from the growth of the post area with medical and school facilities, and from the increase in population density due to migration into the settlement. Most of the other settlements in the SA area are more dispersed (with the exception of KE). While data for two different time points are not available for these settlements, the impression gained from questioning inhabitants is that settlements undergo a similar short-term flux in hamlet composition. While more spatially stable, the population composition of settlements may fluctuate, and sites are occasionally abandoned. The period of flux is measured in months and years for hamlets, years and decades for settlements.

The lability of Semai hamlets and settlements is similar in its basic pattern to the fission-fusion model developed by Neel and his colleagues which was based on South American Indian populations (Neel et al. 1964). I have pointed out this similarity in more detail elsewhere (Fix 1975). The main relevance of this pattern to the concerns of the present work lies in its implications for the study of migration. The continual rearrangement of the population composition leads to a high frequency of migration as measured by birthplaces of resident persons. This, in turn, has implications for other population processes (see chapter 5).

This sketch may serve to introduce the socio-geographically defined levels of Semai society. Further consideration will be given to Semai social life in the next chapter concerning marriage patterns; however, a detailed consideration of Semai culture is beyond the scope of this work. Dentan (1964, 1965, 1968) has already given general ethnographic coverage of the Semai and his works may be consulted for further information.

CHAPTER III

MARRIAGE PATTERNS

In contrast to many preliterate societies, marriage among the SA area Semai is not an occasion for ceremony.[1] The state of being married is thus not always totally clear-cut. Most first marriages for men and women occur when both are young, and could more accurately be considered "affairs". On the average, men and women will have two or three such affairs before entering a more permanent union. The establishment of a liaison can result from mutual attraction of the partners. But if it is to survive any length of time, the girl's parents (especially her father) should approve. With this in mind, young men who are serious about marrying a girl will give gifts to the father and to the girl. There is, however, no formal bride-price.[1]

Marriage Types

This is no ideal Semai pattern of marriage; or rather, the ideal will vary with the speaker and the context in which the pattern is being described. The following types of marriages occur with some frequency.

(1) Marriage of *saiyet* ("children"). In this case, both marriage partners are young, the boy being perhaps thirteen to fourteen, the girl ten or eleven years old. These marriages are almost always of short duration, a few days to a few months, and are looked upon by older people as "play".

(2) Marriage of an older man with a young girl. This is a quite common form. The man may be from fifteen to forty years older

---

[1] See Dentan (1968) for marriage ceremony and *blanja* ("bride-price") among the Western Semai. This pattern is, as Dentan points out, mainly based on Malay wedding practice.

21

than the pre-pubescent girl. The notion is that the man takes over the role of the father; he will *ber-chah* or perform the social duties of fatherhood (e.g., the same word is used of a stepfather, an *abii' berenchah*—the word is derived from *chah*, to eat; *ber-chah*, to feed). Theoretically, the girl when grown will "love you like a father and like a husband" (see Dentan 1965) and will be bound by double ties of feeling. In practice, the usual sequel is for the women to be *kot* or "taken away" by another man more nearly her own age once she is older. It is not uncommon, however, for children to result from these unions and the marriage may persist for many years.

(3) Marriage of a young man and a young girl. This is a less common form of first marriage since both partners will usually have been married as saiyet. Nonetheless, it is the most common beginning of a stable marriage. The age difference between male and female in marriages that have produced offspring is generally not great (see Fig. 3.2C). This type of marriage is often arranged by the girl's relatives. The arrangement does not include formal negotiations between kin groups. It occurs when the girl's relatives, especially her father, extend an invitation to a suitable young man to live with the girl. The extent to which the girl's wishes are taken into account varies. A case was observed in which a thirteen year old girl was promised to a man about ten years older than she. Her response was to move to the house of a young friend. No one came to bring her home nor was any force exerted to compel her to live with the man. After more than a week, she was persuaded to return to her father's house and her new husband. If she had definitely rejected the man, the concerned parties (and anybody else who felt like participating) would hold a meeting *(saguu')* in which the problem would be discussed. In this way, hurt feelings would be relieved and the matter would be closed. The suitor would look elsewhere for a wife. An exactly equivalent procedure is followed for a divorce (see below).

(4) Marriage of a young man with an old woman. There are very few current marriages of this type in existence in the SA area. Several appear in genealogies, however. Many men who survived to a reproductive age without leaving offspring were married to old women beyond menopause. If a man dies at age twenty-five or thirty, while married to a woman of approximately his own age, one or two offspring might be expected to have already been born. This practice in which men marry women either much older or

much younger than themselves can have the effect of lowering the percentage of men contributing offspring to the next generation. Occasionally, a man who is deficient in skills or is physically handicapped may marry an old woman rather than remain single. On the death of his old wife, it is likely that he may not remarry.

In most cases, a young husband survives his wife and remarries. In the one marriage of this kind observed at SA the young husband was actively seeking a younger wife in another settlement. His wife has offspring by her earlier marriage (the oldest of whom is approximately the same age as her husband) by whom she would be supported if divorced. This is, in fact, the most common pattern for old women and men. If, when a spouse dies, the surviving mate is older than fifty years, the offspring are old enough to support their parent. Even when there are no surviving children, relatives are expected to support the old person. According to some reports (Dentan 1968), when food was short or conditions were difficult, old people were sometimes abandoned and left to die. This does not seem to occur now in the SA area.

(5) *Jangar raban*[2]. In a few instances, women are said to have never been married for any length of time to one man but to jangar raban or commit indiscriminate adultery. Extra-marital affairs are not infrequent, (see Dentan 1968) and may lead to divorce. However, after an initial period of experimentation, most women seem to remain married to one man for a considerable proportion of their reproductive years. Those women who do not, appear to be infertile. However, this is only an impression since the number of cases are very few.

(6) Polygamy. The incidence of polygamy in current marriages in the SA area is exceedingly low—two cases only. Both of these occur at BU and both involve older women.

One man of approximately 40 years of age is married to two women, both of whom have children by previous unions. A single child has recently been born to one of these women; the other woman is past childbearing age. This child is the only offspring of the man. The women are in separate settlements; one at KL, the other at BU. The man moves back and forth between them.

---

[2] *Raban* is a Malay word which is translated as "to walk around aimlessly" (Pearce 1944).

The second case involves one old woman past menopause and two old men who are her husbands. As in the first instance, all have been previously married. The polyandrous union is recent and has produced no offspring.

The lack of polygamous marriages is not due to a formal proscription. Several men suggested that they had attempted to set up such unions but in all cases the first wife strongly objected. This resulted either in the divorce of the first wife or in the failure of the husband to take a second wife.

In the past, a few exceptional men seem to have been able to maintain multiple wives in harmony. One man was married to three women for many years and two more for short periods. Four of these wives had a total of twelve offspring, four of which have survived. Another polygamous man, however, had only one child who survived to reproduce. Polygyny, then, is infrequent and does not necessarily result in a large number of offspring.

Figure 3.1 shows the distribution of age differences between spouses for 180 mated pairs from the SA area. Since exact ages could not be assigned to individuals, the differences shown in the figure are in terms of five year age categories. It would, therefore, be possible for a husband-wife pair to differ in age by as much as five years and still be classed in the same age category. Correspondingly, pairs differing by one age category might in fact be only one year apart in actual age (or as much as nine years). Despite these

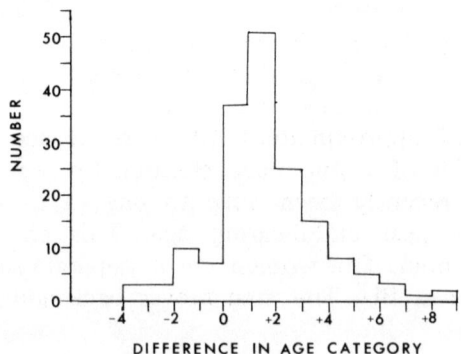

Fig. 3.1 Age differences between spouses by five year categories (male age category +−female age category). Based on 180 marriages.

MARRIAGE PATTERNS 25

limitations, it can be seen that the male is more often the older of the pair; in some cases by as much as forty years.

The overall distribution can be analyzed into three component distributions based on the status of the female. This is done in Figure 3.2. The differences in age between women who have yet to bear children (in general, women younger than eighteen years of age) and their husbands, is large and in all cases the male is the same age or older. This distribution includes many marriages of type 2 discussed above. A sizeable proportion of these marriages

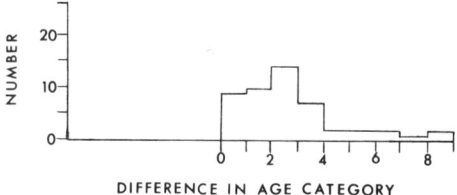

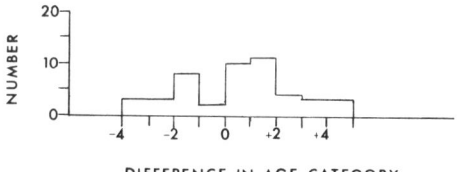

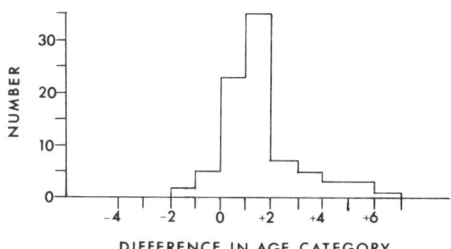

Fig. 3.2 Age differences between spouses
A. First marriage of woman, no children, n=49
B. Second or third marriage of woman, N=47
C. First marriage of woman, with children, N=84.

are recent in origin and many may be expected to end in divorce or in the death of the older male before children are born. The second distribution represents women who have been married at least once prior to their current marriage. These women are older and most have already borne children. Included are several women past the childbearing period whose husbands have died and who have married younger men (marriage type 4).

The third distribution is composed primarily of marriage type 3. The women will probably have been married and divorced as saiyet but their present marriage is the first in which they have borne offspring. In 69 percent of these marriages the husband is in the same age category or one above the wife. Those women in the peak of their childbearing period (age twenty to thirty-five) are generally married to men only slightly older than themselves. Age differentials at first marriages of women are, on the other hand, greater. Women approaching the end of the childbearing period and those women past menopause are more likely to marry men a good deal younger or older than themselves.

An idealized scheme of a woman's marital history might be as follows: A pre-pubescent woman will experience several play marriages with a husband of her own age. She may then be married to a much older man and may bear one or perhaps more children. Through death or divorce this marriage terminates after which she will marry a man a few years her senior. Once children have been born, this marriage may endure for many years. If one spouse dies after their children are grown, it is probable that the surviving spouse will not remarry. If a widow does remarry, she may obtain a mate from a broad range of male age categories. Especially if the woman is older, this new marriage is often unstable. If a widow is still young, remarriage is prompt. The age of the male in this case will generally be approximately the same as the female. The tendency is, then, for women to be married throughout the period of childbearing to males who are not greatly older or younger than themselves.

The marital status of members of the SA area population is shown in Tables 3.1 and 3.2. Despite the probable error in age estimation, the several characteristics of Semai marriage patterns are apparent. When compared to other populations, this distribution is unusual in that in most age categories males greatly outnumber females. (The sex ratio for all ages in Table 3.1 is 1.24; in Table 3.2, it is 1.34.) Detailed consideration will be given to this

MARRIAGE PATTERNS

TABLE 3.1

MARITAL STATUS—LIVING POPULATION
(All settlements except SA.)

Age	Never Married		First Marriage		Second Marriage		Third Marriage		Widowed-Divorced		Total	
	M	F	M	F	M	F	M	F	M	F	M	F
0-15	77	76		13							77	89
15-29	34	1	41	45	1	1		1	2	2	78	50
30-44	2		35	24	10	10	1	2	8	1	56	37
45-49			5	7	14	9	4	1	10	3	33	20
60 +			2			1			3	3	5	4
Total	113	77	83	89	25	21	5	4	23	9	249	200

TABLE 3.2

MARITAL STATUS—LIVING POPULATION OF SA SETTLEMENT

Age	Never Married		First Marriage		Second Marriage		Third Marriage		Widowed-Divorced		Total	
	M	F	M	F	M	F	M	F	M	F	M	F
0- 9	42	29									42	29
10-14	14	8		9							14	17
15-19	17		2	9	1						20	9
20-24			11	7							11	7
25-29	1		10	7	3	4			1		15	11
30-34			5	5	2	3		1	1		8	9
35-39			7	7	2	1	2				11	8
40-44	2		7	4	3	2		2		1	12	9
45-49			2	3	5	1			3	2	10	6
50-55			2	1	2	3	2				6	4
60 +			1	1	2	3	1		3	3	7	7
Total	76	37	47	53	20	17	5	3	8	6	156	116

fact below, but whatever its causes, the implications for marriage patterns are obvious. Proportionally, more females than males are married. Given this sex ratio, marriage types 2 and 4 become more intelligible. If they are to be married at all, some men must either marry old women or young girls. Females thus marry younger, and, as widows, remarry more often than men. As can be seen from the table, almost all women are married by age fifteen. Of the total of 140 females aged 15-44 in Tables 3.1 and 3.2, only three are widowed or divorced, and not yet remarried (these three separations are the results of recent events and the women can be expected to be remarried soon). On the other hand, some 56 men from a total of 209 aged 15-44 (27.5 percent) have either never been married or are not married at present.

A crucial factor limiting the range of potential mates for a male is the shortage of females. Due to this limitation, age restrictions for potential mates are not rigid. Restrictions on the marriage of consanguineous relatives, however, further limits the number of available mates.

Termination of Marriage

Divorce is not an infrequent outcome of the Semai marriage[3]. As was noted above, several types of Semai marriage are unstable. However, if consideration is limited to those matings which have produced offspring, it is found that few end in divorce.

Thus, of the 237 fertile matings ever experienced by living members of the SA area population, 104 have been terminated by the death of one spouse and only 14 by divorce.

Further support for this point is provided by the observation that of the five divorces which occurred during an eight month period at SA, only one involved a couple with children. Moreover, within a month, this marriage was reestablished. The man said that he "yearned for" his children and worried about their food. The children "cried for" their father. The responsibilities and sentiments associated with the rearing of children provided the explicit reasons for the rapprochement.

It is interesting to note that five of the fourteen divorces cited above occurred among parents whose children had died as infants. At the time of divorce, none of the pairs had living children. In two other cases, the marriage produced only one child and in each case the women were remarried while pregnant with the child.

The relatively more common occurrence of divorce among childless couples reduces the chance that one infertile spouse will prevent the other from producing offspring. Since remarriage of a

---

[3] Dentan (1965) found in a case study of 179 marriages (both lowland and highland Semai) that an average of two of every three marriages ended in divorce before one spouse died. Unfortunately, the percentage of these marriages which had produced offspring was not cited.

TABLE 3.3
NUMBER OF PRODUCTIVE MATINGS

Number of Matings	Living Females Age Category					Living Males Age Category				
	15-29	30-44	45-59	60+	Total	15-29	30-44	45-59	60+	Total
1	43	37	16	6	102	38	59	24	5	126
2	5	15	11	1	32	1	9	18	4	32
3		1		1	2					0
Total	48	53	27	8	136	39	68	42	9	158
Average	1.10	1.32	1.41	1.38	1.26	1.02	1.13	1.43	1.44	1.20

woman is usually immediate, no reduction of the total possible progeny results. The trial marriage of young men and girls, while often ending in divorce, occurs in most cases before the girl is old enough to bear children. By the time she is of child-producing age, she will generally have found a suitable mate.

Despite the rarity with which productive marriages end in divorce, many of the women over thirty years of age now living in the SA area have been productively mated more than once. Table 3.3 shows the number of productive matings for both males and females. The lower average for males reflects to some extent the later age at marriage. The factor responsible for the relatively large numbers of both sexes mated more than once is the considerable mortality rate of individuals within the reproductive age span.

Consanguineous Marriage and Inbreeding

Estimates of the amount of inbreeding occurring among the Semai are liable to two main types of error. On the one hand, detailed genealogical knowledge is difficult to obtain. Consequently, much of the inbreeding due to mating between distant kin is unlikely to be discovered. Conversely, there is a tendency on the part of the Semai to lump distant kinsmen together. Thus, it is probable that some individuals living two or more generations in the past may be classed as full sibs when in fact they were cousins. This would tend to increase the estimated level of inbreeding.

These problems are particularly acute since much of the inbreeding appears to be the result of the marriage of fairly distant relatives. The numerical values of F given below are, therefore, only approximate estimates. Thirteen of the eighteen consanguineous marriages at SA involve one particularly extensive genealogy; the pedigree includes eight generations beginning with the ancestor who allegedly "opened" or founded the SA settlement (circa 1800). It is possible (despite repeated cross-checking) that some of the members of a large sibship at the sixth ascending generation level of the genealogy are not sibs but cousins. If so, the SA inbreeding coefficient would be considerably reduced. At the same time, no other genealogy attains this generational depth. Some pairs which were considered to be unrelated might in fact be found to be kin if their more remote ancestry were known.

Since the ancestry of individuals in settlements other than SA is less well known, it is more likely that both types of errors are present in the figures for those settlements. In order to indicate

MARRIAGE PATTERNS 31

the degree of genealogical information upon which the calculations were based, Table 3.4 has been constructed. Information on all four of the grandparents of the spouses is available in only about 55 percent of the marriages. Since the common ancestors in many of the ascertained inbred matings are at the great-grandparent generational level, it may be supposed that much of the remote inbreeding has not been discovered. However, information necessary for the identification of first cousin matings is available for most settlements.

Table 3.5 summarizes the data on consanguineous matings which have produced offspring. Despite the reservations noted above, some general points do emerge from these data. Most conspicuous is the rarity of first cousin marriages. Of the 204 matings for which data on at least two of the spouse's grandparents are known, only two instances of first cousin pairings were found.

TABLE 3.4

GENEALOGICAL INFORMATION
AVAILABLE FOR MATED PAIRS

A. For Matings Having Produced Offspring

	4GPK*	2GPK	PK	I	Total
SA	71	30	6	0	107
	(66.4)	(28.0)	(5.6)		(100.0)
KE	12	7	0	0	19
	(63.2)	(36.8)			(100.0)
RU	13	11	5	1	30
	(43.3)	(36.7)	(16.7)	(3.3)	(100.0)
BU	15	8	8	1	32
	(46.9)	(25.0)	(25.0)	(3.1)	(100.0)
KA	6	8	0	0	14
	(42.8)	(57.2)			(100.0)
CH	12	11	0	0	33
	(52.2)	(47.8)			(100.0)

B. For Matings Not Having Produced Offspring

	4GPK	2GPK	PK	I	Total
SA	18	3	1	0	22
KE	6	1	0	0	7
RU	3	2	0	0	5
BU	4	5	0	0	9
KA	7	1	0	0	8
CH	8	1	2	0	11

*4GPK = All four grandparents of the mated pair known; 2GPK = two grandparents known; PK = parents known; I = incomplete information on the parents of the pair. Percentages are in parentheses

TABLE 3.5
FREQUENCY OF CONSANGUINEOUS MATINGS

Relationship	SA	KE	RU	BU	KA	CH
First Cousins				2		
First Cousins Once Removed					1	1
Second Cousins	5	3	2	1		
Second Cousins Once Removed	10	1			1	2
Double Second Cousins Once Removed						1
Third Cousins	1		1			
Second Cousins + Third Cousins	1					
Second Cousins + Double Third Cousins	2					
Total Inbred	19	4	3	3	2	4
Unrelated	88	15	27	29	12	19
Total	107	19	30	32	14	23
Inbreeding Coefficient	.0022	.0029	.0012	.0044	.0023	.0027

NOTE: Includes only matings which have produced offspring; a portion of these matings are no longer current; i.e., have terminated in divorce or the death of one spouse.

While more remote consanguinity undoubtedly exists undetected, this is less likely in the case of first cousins. Under random mating, the ratio of frequency of first cousin marriages to second cousin marriages varies, depending upon the growth and migration of the population, between 1:2 and 1:4.5 (Hajnal 1963). The ratio for all settlements in the SA area is 2:11 (1:5.5) assuming that the likelihood of discovering a relationship of second cousins with the present data is equivalent to that of first cousins. Furthermore, as Hajnal points out, in most data available, first cousin marriages are more common than second cousin marriages. The ratio for two primitive societies, the Xavante and the Caingang (Salzano et al. 1967) is 4.5:1 and 1:1.6.

A group of young males and females from SA settlement, all unmarried and less than fifteen years old and none of whom were sibs, yielded the ratios in the following table.

From these data on young individuals for whom pedigree information is extensive, it can be seen that the ratio of living cross-sexed cousins is somewhat less than the ratio of marriages of these two types of cousins (average 1:3.5 as opposed to 1:5.5).

TABLE 3.6

RATIOS OF OPPOSITE—SEXED FIRST TO SECOND COUSINS

	Males	Females
Number	21	24
Number of Living Cross-sexed:		
1st C	79	87
2nd C	294	289
Ratio, 1st C:2nd C	1:3.7	1:3.3

This should take on greater significance when it is remembered that it is more likely that some second cousin marriages have not been recognized. This is especially true of BU, the settlement in which both first cousin marriages occur. Unfortunately, the number of marriages is too small to demonstrate unequivocally a lower frequency of first cousin marriage.

It may be supposed that levels of inbreeding in the SA area do not reach those suggested for some other groups at a similar technological level, such as the .02 to .03 for the Xavante (Neel and Salzano 1967). The actual Semai value is undoubtedly higher than that recorded here.

There does not seem to be any preference for either cross or parallel cousins in the few available cases. Of the two first cousin marriages, one is a male mated to his MoBrDa; the other to his MoSiDa. Nine of the sixteen types of second cousin pairings are represented in fourteen cases; no one type occurring more than twice.

A more definite pattern exists for matings between second cousins once removed. In only four of the fourteen cases is the male of the lower generation level. This is not as easily interpreted as the observation that the female is most often of the younger generation for first cousin once removed matings (see Hajnal 1963) since there are a larger number of intervening ancestors. In principle, however, the later age at marriage for males would account for this.

Table 3.7 provides data on extant marriages which have not produced offspring. These marriages are of two sorts: child marriage of type 1, and remarriages of older people beyond the childbearing age, types 2 and 4. Since these marriages are generally unstable, many of those shown in this table will not produce

TABLE 3.7
FREQUENCY OF CONSANGUINEOUS MATINGS

Relationship	SA	KE	RU	BU	KA	CH
First Cousins						
Once Removed		1				
Second Cousins	1	1				
Second Cousins						
Once Removed	1	1			2	1
Third Cousins	4		1		1	1
Total Inbred	6	3	1	0	3	2
Unrelated	16	4	4	9	5	9
Total	22	7	5	9	8	11
Inbreeding Coefficient	.0018	.0078	.0008	.0000	.0014	.0011

NOTE: Matings which have not produced offspring.

offspring. Despite the generally more complete genealogical knowledge concerning the young individuals, the amount of inbreeding is lower in all settlements except KE. The larger value for KE results from one marriage of first cousins once removed. This marriage is interesting in that the age discrepancy between the spouses is large: the man is between fifty and fifty-five years old, the girl about thirteen.

The moderate levels of inbreeding observed in the SA area stem from an ideology of avoidance of consanguineous marriages. This avoidance is not expressed as a strong taboo; no punishment supernatural or otherwise would result. One informant said that the pair might get "sick"[4], but the general view is that the marriage of a relative was simply not a good thing and Semai avoid it. If a young related couple set up a relationship, the concerned parents would *ajar* or "teach" them of their error.

Ideally, no member of an individual's kindred is a potential spouse. Even if the actual ancestral links cannot be traced, if they are suspected to exist the marriage should not be made. Thus, one example was cited in which the great-grandparents of the concerned parties may have been cousins. Informants said that Malay custom would allow the marriage, but Semai of this degree of relationship should not marry. In practice, marriages with

---

[4]Dentan's (1965) informants stated that the *children* of such marriages may be sickly or that there would be a tendency to produce miscarriages and stillbirths.

relatives more distant than first cousins do not provoke an unfavorable community response. A description of the community's response to a marriage of close consanguines has been described by Dentan (1965).

CHAPTER IV

SEMAI AGE AND SEX STRUCTURE

Various attempts have been made to census the aboriginal populations of the Malayan Peninsula ranging from their inclusion in the national census beginning in 1901 to systematic censusing by the Malaysian Department of Aboriginal Affairs (Jabatan Orang Asli) to smaller scale censuses and surveys taken by anthropologists (including the author). In this chapter, the material from some of these sources will be presented and discussed, particularly the data resulting from the 1965 census of aborigines performed by the Jabatan Orang Asli and my census materials collected from the SA area. The aim is to provide the data basic to a later analysis by stable population methods (chapter 6) as well as to present a description of Semai age-sex structure. Some evaluation of the accuracy of the censuses will be made, although a more detailed examination of this problem will be reserved for the stable population analysis.

The report on the national census of 1947 (Tufo 1949) devotes a chapter to the aboriginal tribes including a discussion of the criteria for assigning age and of the difficulties encountered in carrying out the census in the remote and scattered communities of aborigines. Enough description is presented on both of these topics to allow the reader to gauge the severe shortcomings of the census. For example, the instructions to the census-takers for assigning age make it almost a certainty that too many children were classed as under one year, i.e., "children still at the breast but cannot yet walk" (Tufo 1949). Semai mothers nurse their babies to the age of four or older and most one year olds are not yet walking. More serious is the strong likelihood that young females were classed in the older age groups based on the criterion for identifying the ten to fourteen year olds, i.e., "youths and girls

38   THE DEMOGRAPHY OF THE SEMAI SENOI

who are, generally speaking, not yet old enough to be married" (Tufo 1949). Since many Semai girls are married at age twelve or thirteen (see chapter 3), this group will undoubtedly be under-enumerated. Evidence for this age misestimating is provided by the age groups' sex ratio in which the fifteen to twenty-nine year category shows the most females and thus the lowest sex ratio of any class (Tufo 1949).

Likewise, the census totals for Semai must be a large underestimate. Only 7,227 Semai are reported in the 1947 census, compared to 11,609 in the 1960 Jabatan Orang Asli census, implying an annual rate of growth of over 3.5 percent. This may be contrasted to the low growth rates suggested by the total aboriginal census of 1911 to 1947, the highest of which was only about 0.5 percent per year. Table 4.1 also shows an apparent decrease in population from 1921 to 1931 but, as Tufo (1949) points out, this undoubtedly reflects an undercount in 1931. Williams-Hunt (1952) suggested that the actual total of aborigines was a great deal larger than that enumerated in 1947. In all fairness, however, it should be remembered that the uncertainties of the census are carefully specified in the report and, as is noted there, a more accurate census would have required time and money far beyond what was available. Unfortunately, these uncertainties combined with the lack of age distributions for the Semai as a unit make these censuses poor candidates for further analysis.

Some of the same strictures applied to the National Census are also relevant to later censuses conducted by the Jabatan Orang Asli. The actual census schedules, including discussions of criteria for aging, are not available for these censuses. However, it is fairly clear that physiological and life cycle characters were again used to assign ages to persons (see also chapter 5). The major advantage of the Jabatan Orang Asli censuses is that the data are tabulated by

TABLE 4.1

TOTAL NUMBERS OF ABORIGINES ENUMERATED IN THE NATIONAL CENSUSES OF MALAYA, 1911-1947

Census Year	1911	1921	1931	1947
Number	30,065	32,448	31,852	34,737

(from Tufo 1949)

settlement. Therefore, age and sex distributions for the total Semai population as well as subunits of the population may be studied.

Although a complete census was made in 1960, I was able to obtain only those data pertaining to the area studied (SA area). Through the kindness of the Jabatan Orang Asli, I was given access to the entire 1965 Semai census. It is these data which form the basis for many of the calculations in chapter 5.

The total Semai population in 1965 was 12,748 persons, the bulk of whom were living in the states of Perak and Pahang. The only other state with a Semai population was Selangor with fifty-nine resident Semai. As was pointed out in chapter 2, the Semai are not a homogeneous unit in terms of economy and degree of acculturation. By the same token, they are not demographically homogeneous. Those regions with greater access to modern medicine, differing nutrition, and changing attitudes toward age at marriage, etc., may be expected to have experienced a change in mortality rates and perhaps even fertility rates. There is no obvious nonarbitrary method for separating these regions of the Semai population since the degree of acculturation is a continuous variable. Dentan (1965, 1968) has defined cluster areas which are perhaps workable divisions reflecting differing conditions. However, to employ these units would reduce the size of the populations considered. As a compromise, the total Semai population has been divided into two parts in this study. One group includes all those Semai living in Perak state (including Selangor), i.e., the Semai west of the Main Range. The remainder are those to the east in the state of Pahang. This procedure very roughly separates the more acculturated group (West Semai) from the less acculturated (East Semai) (see also Dentan 1968). It is true that the Semai living at the headwaters of the rivers descending from the Main Range in Perak are less influenced by contact than are some Pahang groups. Nonetheless, in general, most of the Western Semai are more acculturated than are the Eastern Semai. The Eastern Semai population should reflect an overall pattern which is closer to the aboriginal condition. The main disadvantages of separating East and West Semai are two: the total population size is smaller (the West Semai number about 9,000; the East, only slightly more than 3,800) and both of the populations may be influenced by migration. This latter objection would have been particularly acute if Dentan's clusters had been used as the units of analysis and would not have been totally excluded even if the total group had been used (see Dentan 1965). As a compromise solution, however, the east-west separation seems justifiable. Migration over the Main Range is not frequent along most of its length and the major effects of acculturation seen in those groups living along roads and near towns in the west are removed.

The population pyramids for the West and East Semai are presented in Figures 4.1 and 4.2, respectively. In these figures, the age distributions are shown as percentages of the total population to facilitate comparison. The corresponding age-sex distributions are provided in Table 4.2.

The most obvious difference between the two distributions is in the percentages of young children: 35.5 percent of the West Semai population is under ten years of age while only 27.4 percent of the East Semai are in this age range. This difference may also be

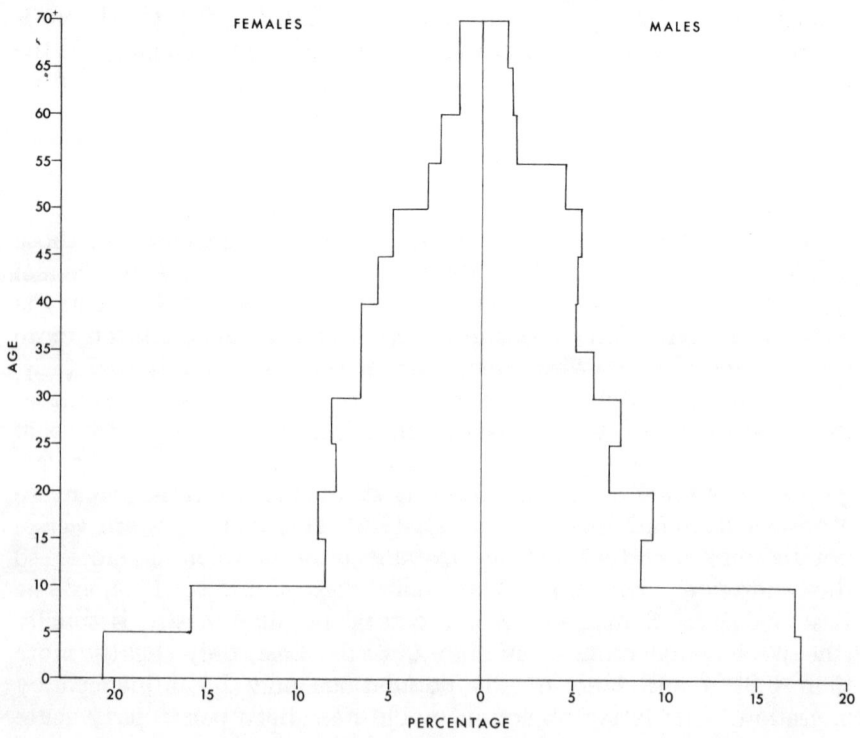

Fig. 4.1 Population pyramid, West Semai, 1965 Jabatan Orang Asli census.

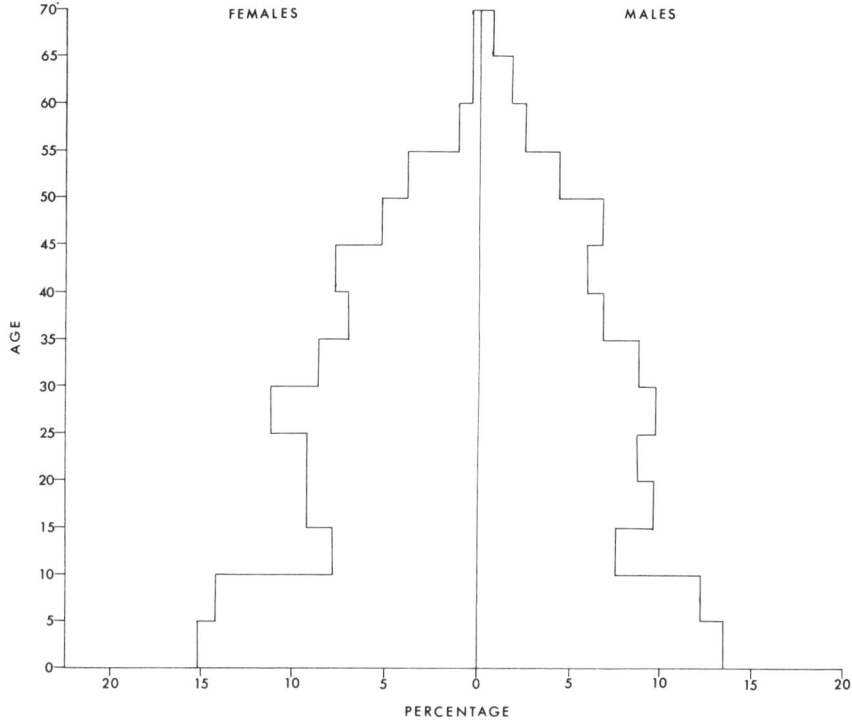

Fig. 4.2 Population pyramid, East Semai, 1965 Jabatan Orang Asli census.

seen in child-woman ratios for the two areas. The ratio of children less than five years of age to women in the reproductive age classes is 0.893 in the west and 0.593 in the east—a substantial difference. Given that the populations are of a relatively large size thus minimizing the likelihood of a difference due to chance and given that the census procedures were similar leading to a similar pattern of age misestimation, a difference of this magnitude seems explainable only as a real difference in basic underlying demographic rates. Since the concern in this work is to arrive at a characterization of the demography of the less acculturated Semai, attention will be focused on the East Semai population.

The East Semai age-sex distribution does not show a regular stepped ascent through the age groups. There is a notable deficiency of individuals in the 10 to 14 year class for both males and

TABLE 4.2
AGE—SEX DISTRIBUTIONS, 1965 CENSUS

	West Semai				East Semai			
	Males		Females		Males		Females	
Age	No.	%	No.	%	No.	%	No.	%
0- 4	759	.175	860	.205	279	.135	262	.151
5- 9	747	.172	658	.157	256	.123	246	.142
10-14	378	.087	350	.084	157	.076	136	.078
15-19	405	.094	369	.088	200	.096	159	.092
20-24	305	.070	330	.079	180	.087	160	.092
25-29	328	.076	338	.081	202	.097	194	.112
30-34	267	.062	272	.065	182	.088	148	.085
35-39	225	.052	271	.065	143	.069	119	.069
40-44	228	.053	233	.056	125	.060	132	.076
45-49	238	.055	196	.047	142	.068	89	.051
50-54	198	.046	122	.029	94	.045	65	.037
55-59	124	.029	92	.022	54	.026	17	.010
60-64	74	.017	49	.012	40	.019	5	.003
65+	57	.015	51	.012	19	.009	5	.003
Total	4,333		4,191		2,073		1,737	

females. It is tempting to ascribe this to the difficult times experienced by the Semai during the Emergency since the years 1950 and 1954 marked the height of the disruption (Polunin 1953). However, this appears less likely when the available (SA area) census materials for 1960 are examined. The shortage of persons 10-14 is also seen here, although it is more pronounced for males in the 5-9 group in both the 1960 and 1965 SA area censuses. Moreover, this is one of the most common patterns of age misestimation found in many other populations (see chapter 6). The irregularity of the rest of the population pyramid also points to age misestimation as a possible explanation for its shape. This conclusion is bolstered by observation of the portions of the 1960 and 1965 censuses covering the SA area. No regular progression of excessive or deficient age groups can be seen going from one age class to the next from the 1960 to the 1965 censuses. The bulge in the ages of peak female reproduction and necking in the 10-14 age classes is apparent in both censuses. Under these circumstances, then, simple inspection of the population pyramid is not sufficient to reveal the demographic history of the East Semai.

Likewise, the temptation to explain the irregularities in terms of history must also be resisted.

In spite of the apparent pattern of age misestimation there are major features ascertainable from the East Semai age-sex structure: (1) the pyramid does not indicate a very young population, yet (2) there are few individuals greater than sixty (particularly females), and (3) the numbers of males exceed those of females at almost every age and particularly in the older age categories (the overall sex ratio is 1.193). The pattern of mortality and fertility determining this age-sex structure will be investigated in detail in chapter 6.

Turning now to my census materials covering a portion of the East Semai population in 1969, a pattern similar to the 1965 Jabatan Orang Asli census can be seen. In this sense, my data are mainly supplementary to the larger body of data from the more inclusive Jabatan Orang Asli census. Still, they are of interest because the pattern (if not the degree) of age misestimation should be different and because they also provide the reference point for the more detailed description of empirically derived demographic rates for the SA area to be presented in the next chapter.

A description of the SA area settlement pattern has already been provided (chapter 2). The census for this area was carried out over a period of several weeks. However, since the number of persons enumerated was relatively small, individuals moving from one settlement to another and persons born or died could be kept track of. Thus, the census date could be roughly standardized at April 15, 1969. A continuous census was kept at the main study settlement (SA) for the eight months of my residence. The population as it existed on April 15 is presented here together with that of the other settlements. Although all the settlements were visited, a few households in two communities were not. Generally, the individuals living in these households were actually seen and their ages estimated by the criteria listed below. In a few cases, individuals and families were visiting elsewhere and age estimates were based on comparisons with resident people. Coverage of the census is, with a small margin of error, complete. This is particularly true in the main study community (SA); it is perhaps less so in one or two of the settlements distant from SA. An added check on completeness is provided by the genealogies. SA settlement individuals have relatives throughout the area. Most of the individuals resident in other settlements had already appeared in SA settlement genealogies prior to the actual census in the other community. Some had visited SA and had been interviewed. Nonetheless, the dispersed settlement pattern and the frequency of short-term visits to other areas make it likely that a few people were missed.

Age estimates of living individuals were made through reference to dated events and comparisons within sib sets. Physiological, behavioral, and life-cycle events are notoriously uncertain indicators of age in populations such as the Semai. The age at which children begin to walk, the age at onset of puberty, and at marriage vary between populations. For this reason, these characteristics or events were treated as only supplementary indicators of age whenever possible.

The local chronology was less detailed than would have been desirable. The most important events were: (1) the 1926 flood during which river levels rose some sixty to eighty feet above normal (Ooi 1963); (2) the short stay of a British officer during the last stages of World War II (circa 1945); and (3) the relocation of some Semai (those north of the SA area) during the Emergency (1950-1952). In addition, the 1960 and 1965 censuses provided a marker for the ages of children born since 1960 and a comparison point for my estimates of older persons (although not a very reliable one).

Relative age is one of the few status markers among the Semai (Dentan 1968) and is reflected in both the sibling and uncle-aunt kinship terminology. Given an order of magnitude (or better) estimate from the dated events, comparisons between sibs or between individuals who knew their ages relative to one another could be made. This was done extensively to bracket ages within smaller bounds.

The degree to which ages are accurate varies with the settlement. For SA settlement, the long period of my residence allowed many age comparisons to be made and estimated ages are probably close to the real figures. Less time was spent in the other settlements and the estimated ages may be assumed to be less accurate. Those individuals whose ages were in the category of "wild guess" (usually persons I did not meet) have been included in the SA area age-sex distribution. However, they amount to only a few percent of the total and should not bias the distribution unduly.

Table 4.3 shows the distribution of the population among the seven settlements of the SA area. The age-sex distribution is shown

SEMAI AGE AND SEX STRUCTURE

TABLE 4.3

DISTRIBUTION OF POPULATION WITHIN THE SA AREA BY SETTLEMENT

Settlement	Population Size (April 15, 1969)
SA	272
KE	69
RU	107
KL	54
BU	107
KA	50
CH	74
Total	733

in Figure 4.3; the relatively more accurately aged SA settlement individuals are represented by the cross-hatched inner pyramid of the figure.

The irregularity of the pyramid is probably due to a combination of age misestimation and real chance fluctuations in these small populations. The deficiency of young females (aged zero to nine) in the SA population, for instance, may be partially a result

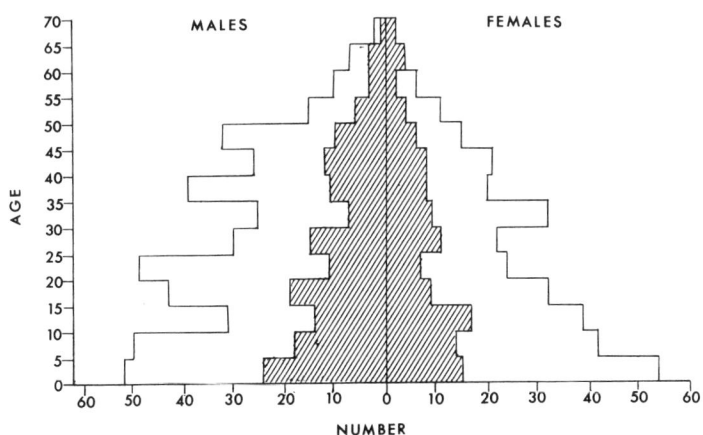

Fig. 4.3 Population pyramid, SA area, N=733. Inner, hatched pyramid, SA settlement, N=272.

of placing a few eight and nine year olds in the 10-14 category, but also may well reflect random events such as a few more male births or a slight excess of young female deaths in recent years. The conspicuous lumping in alternate age categories, particularly in the male population, may be due mainly to age misestimation.

In any case, the basic shape of the pyramid is similar to that of the East Semai as a whole. The different pattern of age misestimation (especially the under-enumeration of 10 to 14 year old females in the East Semai census) makes numerical comparisons inexact, yet the percentages of young and old in the three populations are reasonably close to each other as can be seen in the following table.

TABLE 4.4
COMPARISON OF AGE COMPOSITION OF THE CENSUSES

Census	Percentage less than 15 years old	Percentage greater than 50 years old
SA settlement (1969)	37.5	9.2
SA area (1969)	36.3	8.2
East Semai (1965)	35.1	7.8

The excess of males is also apparent in the SA area population; the sex ratio is 1.276, even higher than for the East Semai census as a whole.

Although the larger size of the East Semai census makes it the more important tool for analysis by stable population methods, the SA area population will be used as a check on inferences derived from it. The SA area age-sex distribution also defines the universe of discussion for the next chapter concerning the demographic rates estimated by the author from field work in this area.

CHAPTER V

DEMOGRAPHY OF THE SA AREA

Several aspects of the demography of the SA area have been examined in preceding chapters including marriage patterns and age-sex structure. The focus of this chapter will be on fertility and mortality measures, migration, and population growth.

The small population size and the lack of long-term records of vital events and of accurate censuses make it almost impossible to obtain great precision and historical depth of the measures. Nonetheless, a general view of Semai demography may be obtained from the available data. This, in turn, may be compared to the demographic picture provided by stable population analysis in the next chapter.

Fertility

A variety of conventional measures of the fertility of a population are available (Barclay 1958). Most are based on the number of recorded births in the year as compared to the total population (the crude birth rate) or to subsets of the total population (usually women in the reproductive age categories), yielding the general fertility rate and/or age-specific birth rates. These rates and ratios may be calculated directly from vital registries and censuses. Another approach is to obtain reproductive histories of women in the reference group. Many of the same measures may be derived from these histories.

A combination of the two approaches will be used in this study. Three censuses are available for at least a part of the SA area, while two, the 1965 and 1969, are available for all the settlements. Although a birth register has not been kept for the Semai, the number of births in the population can be estimated during the period since the 1960 census with some degree of accuracy. From these data child-woman ratios, the crude birthrate and the general fertility rate may be calculated. From the reproductive histories, age-specific birthrates, the total fertility rate and the gross reproduction rate may be derived.

The disadvantage of using recall data is that some pregnancies may not be remembered, especially by older women with many offspring. This tendency to forget should result in underestimates of the true rates. A similar caveat applies to mortality rates derived from recall data. Data from younger women should be more accurate, and therefore those measures which are based on recent events or on the reproductive performance of younger women may give a truer reflection of the demographic pattern. The strategy in this section (as well as that on mortality) will be to present a series of measures which may supplement one another and allow the degree of consistency of the pattern to be gauged.

The simplest measure of fertility is the child-woman ratio, the ratio of the children less than five years of age to the women in the reproductive age categories (15-44) multiplied by a constant (100). This can be calculated directly from one census. For the 1969 SA area population, there are 104 children in the 0-4 age group and 151 women between 15-44 years of age leading to a child-woman ratio of 68.9. This ratio falls in the "high fertility" category as defined by Nag (1962) in his comparative study of fertility in nonindustrial societies. It should be realized, however, that the ratio is very sensitive to errors of age estimation. In addition, it also reflects the mortality pattern of the population. This is particularly relevant to the Semai case since mortality among women of childbearing age is relatively high. A high death rate among the women will decrease the denominator of the ratio and inflate the ratio. This fact limits comparisons to other populations as the measure combines fertility and mortality effects.

The crude birthrate requires more data than are available for the entire SA area. Based on the more detailed and accurate data for SA settlement, the rate is approximately thirty-nine births per 1,000 population. This must be only a rough approximation since it is based on a relatively few births (ninety births since 1960). Interestingly, there were eight births in the period of my residence at SA settlement (October 1968-May 1969) which would suggest a crude birthrate of more than forty-four per 1,000, a figure not greatly larger than the rate based on the longer time span. As Barclay (1958) notes, it is rare to accept a difference in crude rates

DEMOGRAPHY OF THE SA AREA

of less than 10 percent as being valid without careful scrutiny. The margin of error associated with those estimated for the Semai must be greater than that. Given that the birth data for the 1960 and 1969 figure are from individuals' memories (at least for the children born and dying between censuses), 0.039 may be a minimum estimate, the true rate being perhaps slightly more as a general approximation.

The crude birthrate, as the child-woman ratio, is affected by the composition of the population. Age-specific birthrates for women in the reproductive ages are not distorted by variation in age composition and are therefore a more precise measure of fertility. On the other hand, to gain this increased precision, more detailed data are required. Usually the data sources are the censuses and birth registration statistics. It is possible, however, to construct the age-specific fertility schedule from reproductive histories (Barclay 1958). The drawback of this method, as noted before, is that women may underreport the number of children they have borne. In the Semai case, the small number of women for whom reproductive histories are available allows random errors to creep into the data. A total sample of only 117 women may not be truly representative of the fertility of East Semai women in general.

A particularly difficult problem under these circumstances is the calculation of the sterility rate. Clearly with a sample this small, one sterile woman may make a real difference in the percentage. Chance variation in the numbers of nulliparous women between age categories may also influence the calculated age-specific fertility rates. The solution adopted in this study has been to assume an overall sterility rate for the population as a whole. The age-specific estimates of fertility based on women who have borne children is then reduced by this proportion. While admittedly somewhat arbitrary, this procedure should reflect a larger experience than the sample of women available.

Table 5.1 summarizes the data on sterility from the SA area and also from Dentan (1965). Table 5.3 may be consulted for the percentages of childless women for each age category in the SA area sample. The high overall sterility rate for the SA area seems likely to be an artifact of the small sample, especially since Dentan's data on 200 women yielded a much lower rate. On this evidence, the rate obtaining in the older women may be a truer reflection of the average Semai value.

TABLE 5.1

STERILITY IN SEMAI WOMEN
GREATER THAN 20 YEARS OF AGE

Sample	No. of Women	No. Sterile	Percent
Western Semai (Dentan, 1965)	200	3	1.5
SA Area	117	10	8.5
SA Area (Older than 45 years)	28	1	3.6

For younger women (aged 15 to 19), the relatively high percentage (almost 46 percent) who have not yet borne children seems reasonable. Since childbearing seems rarely to begin until about age seventeen or eighteen and approximately one-half of the women in the 15-19 year old category will be below age 17.5, the expected percentage of mothers should be in the neighborhood of 50 percent. Therefore, the observed percentage of childless women in this age range will be used in the calculations which follow.

The calculation of the age-specific rates by the retrospective method depends on estimating the age of the mother at the birth of each of her children. This was accomplished by subtracting the age of living children from the present age of the mother and interpolating for dead siblings of the living children. That is, knowing the birth order of the sibship and possessing estimates of the age at death and year of death of the dead sibs, it is possible to assign a maternal age to the birth of dead offspring. This was done for the entire sample of women. However, estimates for women older than forty-five years proved to be extremely difficult and this group of sixteen women were excluded from the sample.

Table 5.2 shows the results of the calculations for mothers presently aged 15 to 44. The number of children includes all those born at that maternal age to the entire group of women regardless of their present age. The exposure to the risk of childbearing was calculated by assuming that the present age of all the women in a five year category are at the midpoint of the category. For example, all current 20-24 year olds are assigned age 22.5. Since there are fourteen women in this age category, and all were at risk during the entire five year period when aged 15 to 19, these

TABLE 5.2

AGE–SPECIFIC FERTILITY RATES

	Maternal Age					
	15-19	20-24	25-29	30-34	35-39	40-44
No. of Children	82	111	86	46	15	1
Woman-years Exposure	425	370	285	160	103	30
Annual Fertility Rate	.193	.300	.302	.288	.141	.033
Adjusted Rate*	.107	.289	.291	.278	.141	.032

*Adjusted by assuming that 45 percent of women aged 15-19 have not yet borne offspring and an overall sterility rate for the rest of the age classes of 3.6 percent. See text for discussion.

women contribute seventy woman-years of exposure at this maternal age. Only half of the 20-24 year old maternal age category has been passed through by these women, thus, their exposure is thirty-five woman-years. The total exposure at each maternal age was obtained by summing all current age groups.

The gross age-specific fertility rates obtained by this procedure are based on the reproductive performance of women who have borne children. The adjusted rates take into account the presence of some sterile women in the population. The rationale for choosing an overall sterility rate has been discussed above.

The total fertility (completed family size of women surviving to the age of forty-five or more) based on the adjusted age-specific rates is 5.69. In comparison, if *no* sterility occurred (although still assuming approximately half the women aged 15-19 were childless), the total fertility rate would be 5.88. If the observed sterility rates had been used for each age class (see Table 5.3), the total fertility would have been 5.30. Although these values encompass a range of one-half child per woman, they are all of a similar order of magnitude. Moreover, the total fertility rate of 5.69 is, in fact, the completed family size of those SA area women older than forty-five years of age. Table 5.3 shows these data as well as average family sizes for the younger women.

A further check can be made of the reasonableness of the calculated rates. If it may be assumed that the shape of the curve describing the age-specific fertilities (although not the level of fertility), is relatively constant between anthropological populations, the method of Weiss (1973) may be used to construct relative age specific

TABLE 5.3

AVERAGE NUMBER OF CHILDREN BORN TO LIVING WOMEN

Women's Age	15-19	20-24	25-29	30-34	35-39	40-44	45+
No. of Women	24	18	21	19	16	15	28
No. of Children	18	41	70	82	86	71	159
Average per Woman	0.75	2.28	3.34	4.13	5.37	4.73	5.69
Observed Percent Childless Women	45.8	16.7	9.9	5.3	0	20.0	3.6
Adjusted Average per Woman*	0.75	2.63	3.75	4.35	5.18	5.70	5.69

*Adjusted by assuming an average sterility rate of 3.6 percent for the total female population except those aged 15-19.

rates. This involves computing the average of the rates for the seven age classes and then expressing each age-class fertility rate as the product of a constant times this average (see Weiss 1973 for details). These constants may then be compared. Weiss has done this for a series of thirteen anthropological populations. His average values of the constants are compared with those calculated for the Semai in Table 5.4.

Some differences are apparent, but they are quite small. Indeed, there is a remarkable similarity given the range of values among the thirteen populations considered by Weiss.

These rates imply that on the average, about one child is born to women between the ages of twenty and thirty-five every three and one-half years. Before age eighteen, fertility (and perhaps fecundity since most Semai girls are married by age thirteen) is low and after age thirty-nine, fertility drops off sharply. The lack of

TABLE 5.4

AGE—CLASS FERTILITY COEFFICIENTS

	Age Class						
	15-19	20-24	25-29	30-34	35-39	40-44	45-49
Semai	0.66	1.78	1.79	1.71	0.87	0.19	0.00
Average	0.67	1.76	1.76	1.45	0.96	0.33	0.05

children born to young women tends to support the idea that for a period following menarche, girls are relatively infertile (Montagu 1957). Since the sample is quite small and the problems of obtaining exact ages are large, little more may be said. Similarly, the relative infertility of the older women is difficult to explain in a satisfactory manner. However, Table 5.5 provides some data relevant to this question. The range in completed family size is broad and the variance is relatively high. A factor which might be important in lessening the fecundity of older women (and thus increasing the variance in family size) is the prevalence of disease associated with childbearing. Infection and trauma after several births may lower the possibility of conception or render a woman sterile. Further discussion will be devoted to maternal illness below.

It is tempting to speculate that the recent hypothesis of Frisch and McArthur (1974) relating the nursing of offspring, body weight, and amenorrhea may explain the relatively long space between births. That is, nursing mothers require additional calories to maintain their weight (perhaps as much as 1,000 calories per day extra). If these additional calories are not available and the weight falls below a critical threshold, ovulation does not take place. Semai women breast feed their children for up to three or four years. Several studies have shown that lactation inhibits conception (Jain et al. 1970); the Frisch-McArthur hypothesis would account for these observations in a reasonable fashion. It may also be relevant to the period of adolescent infertility. However, in the absence of data on the weights of nursing mothers and the establishment of the threshold for the Semai, this must remain speculation.

Two other factors which have been suggested as possible birth spacing mechanisms may be excluded with a fair degree of

TABLE 5.5

COMPLETED FAMILY SIZES

No. of Women	Number of Offspring												
	0	1	2	3	4	5	6	7	8	9	10	11	$\bar{x}$	σ^2
28	1	1	1	0	5	5	5	5	2	1	1	1	5.69	6.00

confidence; post-partum sex taboo and abortion/infanticide. Post-partum sex taboos would delay conception by an insignificant length of time in the case of the Semai since coitus begins "as soon as the woman feels like it," a variable, but not particularly long time after the birth of the child. Sex is also taboo during sickness, but again this varies in duration and is usually an insignificant period.

Although abortion and infanticide cannot be totally excluded as birth spacing alternatives among the Semai, all indications are that these are most probably not occurring. Intensive questioning yielded no information on abortifacients of any type. According to one of my best informants (an old woman who was also a midwife) abortion was simply not practiced. This opinion seemed general. Infanticide, too, runs counter to Semai sensibilities. In a western Semai village, people learned of the abandonment of a child by an Indian mother; they were horrified. Occasionally, a Semai mother will give her child to a sister or other woman who is childless, but she will not destroy it. This is the solution generally adopted in the event of twin births, also. The child is given to a relative to raise. Infanticide and/or abortion, while important in many societies, (Birdsell 1968) are probably nonexistent or of extremely low frequency among the Semai.

While premeditated infanticide does not occur among the Semai, a sort of infanticide by neglect may be of importance in limiting the number of surviving infants. The Semai exhibit a fatalism concerning children that are sickly or malnourished due to failure of lactation in the mother (see also Lorimer et. al. 1954; Beals, Spindler and Spindler 1973). One case observed concerned an infant whose mother became sick after its birth. She did not have enough milk to feed the child. Rather than find a wet nurse, the child was fed powdered milk. The attitude of the parents toward the child appeared apathetic. The child became emaciated and might not have survived if the woman had not finally been convinced to go to the hospital. After good care and feeding, the child became much more healthy looking and the parents showed much more interest in it. This is not to say that Semai are generally not willing parents. But in some cases, the use of a wet nurse (which does not seem to occur) or a less fatalistic attitude might result in increased survival rates of children.

Mortality

As in the case of fertility measures, a variety of methods of studying mortality exist (Barclay 1958). Several are analogous to the rates and ratios used in fertility analysis, in that the numbers of events are related to the base population. These include the crude death rate, infant death rate, and age-specific death rates. In addition, a more detailed method, the life table, can be applied to the analysis of mortality. Again, as with fertility information, much of the data on mortality are of the retrospective variety gained from genealogies and reproductive histories. The 1960, 1965 and 1969 censuses will also be used to define base populations and to determine which individuals died between censuses.

Perhaps the most common summary measure of the mortality experienced by a population is the crude death rate, the ratio of deaths for a specified period (usually one year) to the mid-period (mid-year) population (Barclay 1958). As was the case for the crude birthrate, sufficient data for the calculation of the crude death rate are available only for SA settlement. Based on the number of deaths since 1960 (as determined by the censuses, reproductive histories, and genealogies) and the mid-period population estimate, the crude death rate is in the neighborhood of 30 deaths per 1,000 population, as figured on an annual basis. The same caution must be used in interpreting this rate as was applied to the crude birthrate. This must be a minimum estimate since the likelihood of failing to ascertain a death which occurred during the reference period is greater than that of erroneously recording a death. Indeed, I have been unable to account for eight individuals listed on the 1960 SA settlement census; if they died rather than migrated to another settlement, the total number of deaths would rise to 78 and, correspondingly, the crude death rate would reach 33 per 1,000.

Another method of showing mortality in the absence of a system of vital registration is to compare the survival rates of offspring of women of completed fertility (Neel and Chagnon 1968). The data on total number of live births has already been presented (Table 5.5). Table 5.6 shows the number of surviving offspring of those women. The difference in means (2.93 compared with 5.69) indicates considerable mortality; almost one-half of the live born offspring of these women have failed to survive.

TABLE 5.6
SURVIVING OFFSPRING OF WOMEN OF COMPLETED FERTILITY

No. of Women	Number of Offspring								
	0	1	2	3	4	5	6	$\bar{x}$	σ^2
28	2	4	8	3	5	3	3	2.93	2.59

This figure, however, represents the survival of offspring to varying ages. Thus, some sibships include individuals as old as forty years while others include prereproductive age children. Clearly, a more specific measure would be advantageous.

William Brass has worked out an ingenious method for estimating mortality based on the survival of offspring and maternal age (Brass et al. 1968, U.N. 1967). Briefly, according to Brass, the mortality for each age group can be estimated from the proportion of offspring dead among those ever born to women of a specified age group. A correction factor is applied to compensate for the age at which fertility begins in the population. Table 5.7 which follows presents these estimates for the SA Semai. The correction factor has been applied for a median age of the fertility schedule of 27.7 years.

With the exception of the first and last figures (proportions dying before age one and before age fifteen), these estimates exhibit a consistent pattern of decreasing survivors. According to

TABLE 5.7
MORTALITY ESTIMATES—BRASS METHOD

Age (x)	Proportions Dying*	Proportions Surviving	Mothers' Age (m)
1	.356	.644	15-19
2	.297	.703	20-24
3	.346	.654	25-29
5	.381	.619	30-34
10	.425	.575	35-39
15	.415	.585	40-44

*Proportion of children dying before age x estimated from survival of offspring of mothers in age group m.

TABLE 5.8

INFANT DEATH RATES

Birth Cohort	Male	Female
1960-64	250	200
1965-69	280	235
Average	264	216

Brass, the deaths of infants aged less than one year estimated from child survival of 15-19 year old women "should not be regarded seriously because of the basic weakness of the method of estimation at this point" (U.N. 1967). Part of the difficulty in the Semai case is that offspring survival of these young inexperienced mothers seems lower than in older mothers, a violation of one of the basic conditions of the method (U.N. 1967). In general, the best estimate of infant mortality may be derived from the proportions surviving to age two and accepting the relationship between survival to age two and survival to age one in a model life table. This will be done in chapter 6. The increase in survival proportions from age ten to age fifteen is quite small and may be simply an artifact of the data. The estimates imply that 70 percent of the children survive to age two and between 55 and 60 percent survive to age fifteen. They are consistent with the rough approximations of survivorship already presented.

Age-specific rates of death may also be calculated from the available data, i.e., a record of deaths over the last twenty years and an estimate of the population sizes of each age class at the midpoint of the period.

Death rates for infants (less than one year old) expressed as the ratio of infant deaths to the number of births for a specified unit of time, $(d_0/b)k$ (where k=1000), are shown in Table 5.8. These rates are based on a total of ninety births and twenty-two deaths for the 1960 to 1969 period.

Death rates for the older ages were computed on the basis of deaths over a twenty year span. Deaths occurring in the decade prior to the 1960 census are less certain to have been included. But even this sacrifice of precision was able to increase the number of events to only ninety-five. Clearly, the small differences in the numerical values in the following table cannot allow for much interpretation.

TABLE 5.9
AGE SPECIFIC DEATH RATES

Age Group	Males	Females	Total
1-4	23.5	31.8	26.8
5-14	8.6	3.6	6.1
15-24	9.3	10.0	9.5
25-34	22.5	25.0	23.6
35-44	20.0	25.0	22.2
45-54	39.0	39.0	39.0
55-64	41.6	63.5	50.0
Total	19.4	21.0	20.2

NOTE: Deaths per 1,000 population. $\frac{d_i}{P_i} k$; where d_i is the number of deaths in the ith age grouping per "year," P_i is the midyear population in the same age group, and k is 1,000. d_i was obtained by dividing the number of deaths by twenty. The midyear population was taken to be that of 1960. The present (1969) age structure was projected on the population size of 1960 (248 individuals) to obtain p_i. This was compared to the actual age structure as recorded in the 1960 census; the results were approximately the same.

A further difficulty in arriving at these estimates should be mentioned. Numerous problems exist in estimating the ages of living Semai; these are compounded when dead individuals are considered. Behavioral characteristics such as "crawling," "sitting-up," "standing" and "walking" had to be used to estimate the infants' ages at death. Older children and adults' ages at death were obtained by a combination of comparisons with living children, reference to dated events, comparisons with sib sets, and estimated age on the 1960 and/or 1965 censuses (see the earlier discussion of aging). All of these techniques together may place the age estimates at approximately the right order of magnitude. But the precision provided by registered vital events and known ages is lacking in these data.

With these cautions in mind, it may still be interesting to examine an abbreviated life table derived from the age-specific death rates. This may later be compared to the life tables obtained by stable population methods.

The basic parameters to be estimated for the life table are the mortality rates ($_n q_x$). The accepted method of estimating the life table mortality rates from age-specific death rates is:

$$_n q_x = \frac{2 n_n M_x}{2 + n_n M_x}$$

where n is the number of years in the age category, and $_nM_x$ is the age-specific annual death rate for that age category x to x+ n (Barclay 1958). Given $_nq_x$, $_np_x$, the survival rate is simply $1 - {_nq_x}$; and l_x, the proportion of an initial cohort l_0 ($l_0 = 100$ in Table 5.10) surviving to exact age x, is calculated as $l_{x+n} = l_x\, {_np_x}$.

Despite all the reservations and qualifications which must be made concerning the quality of the data, the pattern expressed by the age-specific rates is both consistent with the estimates of mortality already derived and is similar in shape to the general curve of mortality found in most human populations. Indeed, as will be shown in the next chapter, these rates are not strikingly different from those predicted on the basis of stable population analysis (see Figure 6.4). As is universally true, the infant death rate is high in comparison with the other ages; mortality falls to a minimum in the ages five to ten and gradually increases through the later ages.

In terms of the Semai pattern in particular, the infant death rate is high by national population standards but not very high in comparison with other anthropological populations (Weiss 1973). Indeed, as Barclay (1958) notes, infant death rates of 250 to 300 per 1,000 were once typical of most populations. The Semai

TABLE 5.10

ABRIDGED SEMAI LIFE TABLE

Age	Males			Females		
	$_nq_x$	$_np_x$	l_x	$_nq_x$	$_np_x$	l_x
0	.234	.766	100.0	.197	.803	100.0
1	.111	.889	76.6	.119	.881	80.0
5	.042	.958	68.2	.018	.982	70.7
10	.042	.958	65.3	.018	.982	69.5
15	.045	.955	62.6	.049	.951	68.2
20	.045	.955	59.8	.049	.951	64.9
25	.107	.893	57.1	.118	.882	61.7
30	.107	.893	51.0	.118	.882	54.4
35	.095	.905	45.5	.118	.882	44.6
40	.095	.905	41.2	.118	.882	39.4
45	.178	.822	37.3	.178	.822	34.7
50	.178	.822	30.6	.178	.822	28.5
55	.188	.812	25.2	.274	.726	23.5
60	.188	.812	20.5	.274	.726	17.1
65			16.6			12.4

recognize the rather high likelihood that a child will not reach his first birthday and do not name their children during the first months of life.

Mortality during the ages one to four is only moderately high. By the time a child begins to walk, his chances of survival are much improved. Sickness and death associated with weaning does not seem to be as much of a problem as has been suggested elsewhere (Dubos 1965).

Throughout the period from five to twenty-four years of age, the death rate again is moderate. During the reproductive period, a not inconsiderable number of deaths occur. It is tempting to attribute the higher rate for women to the hazards of childbearing. This will be discussed further in the next section.

Causes of Death

According to the Semai, infectious disease is the single most important cause of death. Death due to wild animals, snakes, accidents, homicide, suicide, raiding—all these are nonexistent or exceedingly rare. Very occasionally an individual is said to have died due to old age (*chukop umor*). Table 5.11 gives an indication

TABLE 5.11

CAUSES OF DEATH*—ALL SETTLEMENTS—1950-1969

	0-1 M	0-1 F	1-14 M	1-14 F	15-44 M	15-44 F	45+ M	45+ F	Total M	Total F
Respiratory	12	4	4	1	3	2	8	6	27	13
Dysentery	2		2		10	7	4	2	18	9
Diarrhea	1	2	5	2	1				7	4
Barah	1			2	1	2	1		3	4
Fever	1		1		1	1	1	1	4	2
Sampuu'	10	16	5	5					15	21
Accident						1	2		2	1
Loss of Mother	6	3							6	3
Died 1 week old	11	6							11	6
Childbirth						13			0	13
Other	2		1				1		4	0
Unknown	45	30	11	14	11	3	6	8	73	55
Total	91	61	29	24	27	29	23	17	170	131
Sex Ratio	1.49		1.21		0.93		1.35		1.30	
Percent	50.5		17.6		18.6		13.3		100.0	

*See text for explanation of categories.

of the types of diseases which are responsible for some 300 deaths in the SA area in the last twenty years.[1]

The diagnosis of these diseases is approximate to say the least. Perhaps most of the categories listed should be included in the already substantial grouping "unknown." Semai disease categories tend not to be coterminous with those of Western medicine except in a few cases. Especially in the case of small children, the usual response to questions about the cause of death was that "we don't know—kids just die."

The most common cause of infant death given by informants was *sampuu'*, a word of Malay origin but uncertain referent. Wilkinson (1932) translates it as "debility; wasting sickness." According to the Semai, the symptoms of death due to sampuu' were paleness and a "deficiency of blood" (*kurang behiib*).[2] From this information, an unequivocal diagnosis is difficult.

It is somewhat surprising that so few infant deaths were reportedly due to "fever." Malaria is certainly prevalent in the SA area (see below). It is probable that some deaths from malaria do occur but the frequency cannot be estimated from my data.

Respiratory diseases are responsible for a large number of deaths. In childhood, *siih* is most common. Generally siih is fairly mild and appears to be equivalent to the common cold. But more severe diseases such as influenza and pneumonia seem to be lumped in this category.

The relatively large number of infants dying less than one week after birth (17 of 152 infant deaths) may be attributable to premature births. This is made plausible by Bolton's statement (1968) that 30 percent of aborigine births at Gombak Hospital are premature and 5 percent are under four pounds in weight.

Another source of neonatal and early infant mortality is the death of the mother or her failure to lactate. The latter is particularly evident in young mothers. One case was observed during my residence at SA settlement; the child would almost certainly have died if the mother had not been convinced to take it to the hospital. As will be suggested below, mortality in childbirth is not uncommon. Although surviving children of such

---

[1] Sample sizes for different attributes may vary. Thus data on "cause of death" does not require precise estimates of age at death nor of the population composition. Therefore, deaths occurring in all settlements could be used.

[2] A shortage of blood seems to be a Semai indication of poor health. Thus healthy people have lots of blood; unhealthy ones do not.

women are occasionally adopted by other women (this was observed at SA), often the child does not survive.

As in infants, respiratory disease is a major source of mortality in adults. Many adult Semai exhibit signs of pulmonary problems: rapid breathing, rasping sounds, coughs, etc. Again, it appears that several diseases are involved. Tuberculosis is fairly common in aborigines (Bolton 1968), though bronchitis probably makes up the major portion of the category the Semai call *senloot*. It may also be true that some individuals died *with* rather than *of* *senloot*.

A Semai disease which may correspond rather well with a Western category is *choh behiib*, amoebic dysentery. The Semai word means literally "bloody stool." This disease is especially common at SA settlement. The incidence is lower in more remote settlements. It may be that amoebiasis is a fairly recent disease in the SA area.

A variety of other diseases cause a few deaths each. *Barah* is a Malay word and refers to an abcess (Wilkinson 1932). Swellings of the stomach and abdominal region are the major Semai symptoms of barah. Accidents are mainly due to falls which often occur while climbing trees for fruit. One case of what might have been leprosy was recorded.

Death due to problems at childbirth accounts for a relatively great number of female deaths in the reproductive ages (almost 45 percent). The usual complication according to the Semai is retained placenta, i.e., "the child's house does not come out." Infections probably also play a role in maternal mortality. One of the four births which took place at SA settlement during our residence was followed by such an infection. It is significant that an absolutely larger number of women than men in this age category have died even though the sex ratio of the cohort entering the category was high. Clearly, maternal mortality has a large impact on the female population.[3]

Since more than 40 percent of the deaths recorded in Table 5.11 are due to unknown causes, generalizations are difficult to make. Almost certainly malaria is more common than indicated in these statistics. A survey conducted by Dr. James Chin at SA

---

[3] Dr. Frederick Dunn who has much experience with Malayan Aborigines feels that maternal deaths are not uncommon in other aborigine groups (personal communication).

settlement in 1963 showed a blood smear parasite rate of 21.6 percent (personal communication). On the other hand, a disease which is much more important in other Semai areas, infectious hepatitis (Dentan 1968), may be less so in the SA area. Jaundice *(nyi' rement)* is not uncommon but no deaths were attributed to it.

A thorough treatment of Semai disease patterns is beyond the scope of this study and beyond my competence. Fortunately, such a study already exists (Polunin 1953). Bolton (1968) also summarizes disease patterns of the Malayan aborigines in general and Dentan (1965, 1968) provides further material as well as a really excellent interpretation of Semai beliefs about disease. Furthermore, Dentan (1965) describes the process of childbirth; a subject relevant to maternal mortality.

Migration

Migration is a topic of interest to both demographers and geneticists as it affects the age-sex structure and the distribution of population and, at the same time, the distribution and frequency of genes. I have already devoted some consideration to local migration and its effect on gene frequencies elsewhere (Fix & Lie-Injo 1975) and, therefore, will not deal with that subject in detail here. However, as migration affects measures such as annual rates of growth and the age-sex composition of the population, an attempt to gauge its magnitude will be made.

In contrast to most other measures in demography, migration statistics are not easily standardized in counting units (Barclay 1958). The line between visitors and migrants, for instance, is not always easy to draw. This is particularly true in populations such as the Semai where local settlements are quite labile in composition (for example, see the section in chapter 2 on the changing hamlet composition at SA settlement).

In addition, the territorial scope of the migration is important in defining a migrant. Depending on the interests of the investigator, this may range from international migration to local settlement units. For the Semai, international migration is not relevant, although some West Semai women have married Chinese men and a very few Indians. Of principal concern is the movement of people between settlements, in and out of the SA area and the ethnic group as a whole.

A third problem in the analysis of migration involves the type of statistics to be employed. The conventional types are transit statistics, records of people passing some port of entry, and census statistics by place of birth. The first of these requires some on-going record keeping of movement or a survey of individuals' migrational histories. Only the survey method is possible for the Semai. Place of birth data are available for all Semai in my census and were also included on the 1965 Jabatan Orang Asli census. However, there are two difficulties associated with the 1965 census data. One is that they are not very accurate. Extensive cross-checking between the 1965 census and my data for the SA area shows many errors. The routine adopted by the census takers appeared to be to assign the present place of residence as the birthplace of the individual. Secondly, the definition of birthplace differs between individuals. Some gave the name of a small tributary or stream along which their parents were living at the time of their birth. Others gave the name of a major river valley encompassing many distinct settlements. Where I am familiar with the local places, it is possible to take these differences into account. For other areas covered by the 1965 census, however, it is difficult to determine the degree of error. The percentages of individuals born elsewhere than the censused community seem to vary within similar limits in the known SA area communities and elsewhere in the East Semai area. Since there are no obvious inconsistencies between the 1965 census birthplaces recorded for the SA area and elsewhere, my more accurate data from the SA area will be examined.

Looking first at the data for SA settlement, it will be seen that even though the frequency of migration is high, the net change in population size may be low. Table 5.12 shows migration into and out of SA settlement between the 1960 census and my census of 1969. In-migrants are those individuals now resident at SA settlement who were nonresident in 1960; out-migrants are those who left SA settlement between 1960 and 1969. The net change is in terms of the 1969 SA population. A "+" represents an addition to the 1969 population, "-", a subtraction.

Thus a turn-over of more than 10 percent of the population in the last ten years has resulted in a net increase in population size of only two individuals. However, this does not take into account age differences between in- and out-migrants. Women in fertile age classes may have significant effects on the population

DEMOGRAPHY OF THE SA AREA

TABLE 5.12

MIGRATION, SA SETTLEMENT, 1960-69

	In-Migrants		Out-Migrants		Net Change	
	Males	Females	Males	Females	Males	Females
Movement within SA area	13	8	14	8	-1	0
Movement outside SA area	5	4	5	1	0	+3
Total	18	12	19	9	-1	+3

either by adding or removing their potential offspring from the population. As will be seen in the next section, this has had an impact on apparent population growth in SA settlement. Furthermore, SA settlement may be atypical of the settlements in the area in showing little net change in population due to migration. Unfortunately, the 1960-69 statistics for the other settlements do not allow a similar in-migrant/out-migrant analysis.

It is possible to analyze the birthplace data for most of the SA area settlements. Table 5.13 indicates some variability in the percentages of migrants defined on the basis of birthplace. These data include all generations of the resident populations and, therefore, migrants may be recent or longtime residents of the settlement. Tables 5.14 and 5.15 highlight other aspects of the pattern of migration, focusing on married pairs and parent-offspring dyads respectively. All three tables indicate a considerable frequency of migration. The variation between settlements ranges from the KA population in which 86 percent were born elsewhere to the SA settlement in which only 30 percent were migrants. Likewise, only 5½ percent of the resident RU married pairs were composed of two individuals born in RU. This represents a considerable influx of migrants into RU in the last fifteen years (see Fix 1975). Parent-offspring birthplaces range from those in which more than 70 percent of the children are born in the same settlement as their parents (at CH), to those in which less than 12

TABLE 5.13

BIRTHPLACES OF THE SA AREA POPULATION

Settlement	N_r	Within Settlement	Within SA Area	Outside SA Area	Unknown
SA	272	.702	.948	.052	0
KE	69	.536	.912	.051	.029
RU	107	.486	.673	.327	.009
KL	54	.444	.593	.185	.222
BU	107	.626	.934	.057	.009
KA	50	.140	.580	.380	.040
CH	74	.677	.855	.145	0

NOTE: Decimal figures are the fractions of the resident populations, N_r, born (1) within the settlement of residence, (2) within the SA area which includes the persons born within the settlement of residence, those born in other settlements in the SA area, as well as a few older individuals born in now abandoned settlements located within the geographic SA area, and (3) in settlements outside the SA area.

TABLE 5.14

BIRTHPLACES OF MARRIED PAIRS

Settlement	N	Within Settlement	Within SA Area	Outside SA Area
SA	117	.453	.888	.112
KE	19	.210	.946	.054
RU	37	.054	.648	.352
KL	34	.147	.824	.176
BU	33	.182	.847	.153
CH	79	.304	.721	.279

NOTE: Based on data from 345 marriages. For the 319 marriages presented here, at least one of the spouses was born in the SA area. In an additional twenty-seven marriages (7.8 percent of the total) neither spouse was born in the SA area. The column headed "N" gives the number of marriages in which one of the spouses was born in the settlement indicated (either the husband or the wife was arbitrarily chosen as the reference individual except when one or the other was born outside the SA area). In order to increase the sample of marriages, marriages in which one of the spouses is dead but with known birthplace were included. Only six married individuals were born at KA; therefore, this small settlement is not included in the table.

DEMOGRAPHY OF THE SA AREA

TABLE 5.15

PARENT—OFFSPRING BIRTHPLACES

		Birthplaces		
Settlement	N	Within Settlement	Within SA Area	Outside SA Area
SA	449	.601	.992	.078
KE	82	.171	.915	.085
RU	114	.298	.526	.474
KL	70	.430	.687	.313
BU	139	.575	.870	.130
KA	26	.115	.577	.423
CH	153	.705	.871	.129

NOTE: Based on both father-offspring and mother-offspring birthplaces. The column "N" gives the number of parent-offspring pairs. The values represent the fractions of offspring born in the settlement listed under the "settlement" column having a parent born (1) in the same settlement, (2) in the same settlement or in another SA area settlement or (3) in a settlement located outside the SA area. (See Fix & Lie-Injo 1975, for detailed migration matrix).

percent are at KA. This variability is due to the continual rearrangement of the population composition of settlements, the fission-fusion structure of the Semai (Fix 1975). Some settlements have recently gained fusion groups (particularly KE, RU, and KA), while others have not. Although this structure has many implications for the genetics of local populations (Neel 1967), the main import of fission and fusion for the demography of the Semai lies in the effects on the calculation of growth rates and other measures presupposing a closed population. An assumption of stable population analysis, for instance, is that the population is closed to migration. In this connection, it is interesting to note that migration, while frequent between settlements, is not nearly as high to and from settlements outside the SA area. Moreover, the bulk of the outside migration occurs with a few settlements to the north of the SA area. Only one settlement (BU) has received in-migrants from across the Main Range, the dividing line between what I have termed the West and East Semai. The frequency of this West-East migration has been quite low even in this settlement; only two married women were born across the Main Range. There is probably more mate exchange and migration across the Main Range farther north in Semai country, but it would appear that the East Semai population may be relatively isolated from the West. This is less true for the SA area. Except over the short-term, settlements are not closed to migration.

Population Growth

Population growth results from the interaction of the processes already described: fertility, mortality and migration. In a closed population, an excess of births over deaths leads to growth (growth equals births minus deaths). In any particular population, however, in- and out-migration may play a greater role in promoting or retarding apparent population growth than do births and deaths. The data presented in the last section indicate that this would be true for most Semai settlement populations. The problem, then, is to separate the growth rate implied by mortality and fertility rates (the so-called "intrinsic" rate of natural increase) from the overall growth rate as it is influenced by migration. Although both quantities are of interest, the growth rate is subject to larger fluctuations over a shorter time period as migrants come and go. The rate of natural increase may also vary between local groups as a result of chance variations in rates. But it is representative of underlying biological processes which vary less radically than does migration. Moreover, it is the intrinsic rate which ties the empirical observations to the theory of stable populations.

The basic equation of population growth is:

$$P_2 = P_1 e^{rn}$$

population size at time 2 (P_2) is equal to the initial population size (P_1) times a growth factor—an exponential, since growth is a compound interest process, r being the rate of growth and n being the number of years between time 1 and time 2.

In order to find the growth rate, all the data that are required are population figures from two censuses (assuming that the area and completeness of coverage are comparable). These data are available for the Semai as a whole, the SA area, and SA settlement.

These figures suggest that the SA area population is growing at a fairly high rate; the population would double in about thirty-six years growing at the annual rate of 0.0193. However, a number of factors may inflate these estimates. The small number

TABLE 5.16

ANNUAL RATES OF GROWTH

Population	Population Size			Rate of Growth	
	1960	1965	1969	1960-65	1960-69
All Semai	11,609	12,748		.0187	
SA Area*	507	539	603	.0122	.0193
SA Settlement	248	259	272	.0087	.0103

*1960 census data available for only four of the seven settlements.

of individuals involved magnifies errors. A slight under-count in the 1960 census coupled with a more complete enumeration in 1969 could make a rather large difference in the estimated rate. For example, only forty-four people need to have been missed in the 1960 census in order for the 1960-69 SA area growth rate to be almost halved ($r=0.01$). Since an under-enumeration is more likely to have occurred than an over-enumeration, the growth rates in Table 5.16 are maximum estimates (assuming that my 1969 census was complete).

These growth rates are probably not suitable as measures of intrinsic rates of increase. The frequent migration documented in the preceding section could have significant effects on the rate of growth in the SA area. For instance, the large number of young married migrants at RU are now producing many children. This raises the apparent rate of population growth.

When migrants are removed from the 1960-69 base populations, the growth rate is lowered. Some 461 of the 507 persons appearing on the 1960 SA area census are either still within the SA area or died within the SA area. Approximately 131 living children have been born since 1960. Subtracting the deaths and adding the children, results in a 1969 natural population of 490. The growth rate unaffected by migration in the SA area from 1960 to 1969 then equals 0.0068 or about 0.7 percent per annum. Since there is considerable opportunity for error in this procedure (especially in deciding whether some of the individuals on the 1960 census died or migrated elsewhere) and since the numbers involved are small, this figure should be interpreted cautiously.

At the same time, the crude rate of increase (the difference between the crude birth and death rates) is quite similar to this value. Depending on whether the death rate of 30 per 1,000 or 33 per 1,000 is accepted, the rate of increase is either 9 per 1,000 or 6 per 1,000 (0.9 percent or 0.6 percent). These figures bracket the value obtained from the adjusted census figures.

Further perspective and some comparative data on population growth will be provided in the next chapter. It may be pointed out here, however, that a growth rate of even 0.7 percent per year would lead to a very large population over the long term. For example, the 1965 Semai population of 12,748 growing at an annual rate of 0.7 percent would reach a population size of nearly 14 million in 1,000 years. It may be assumed that the Semai have not always been growing at this rate. It is more probable that short-term growth might be followed by a decrease with considerable fluctuation in local populations.

In the future, if the experience of the SA area population follows that of their cohorts in the more acculturated western portion of the Semai distribution, effective fertility may be expected to increase and mortality decrease as they come more into contact with medical service. What may be a most striking trend is the increasing desire of SA women to give birth in the hospital. Of the eight births recorded at SA settlement during the period of residence there, five took place in the hosptial.[4] This should result in a decrease in maternal sickness and death and peri-natal infant mortality. Moreover, those women with hospital experience are more likely to take their sick children back for medical care. At least two deaths were averted by medical care in my eight months of observation.

The Semai, then, may be approaching a stage in which their population will be growing at a rate similar to that of the rest of the Malaysian population, i.e., more than 3 percent per year (Keyfitz and Fleiger 1971).

---

[4]The Orang Asli hospital at Ulu Gombak (See Bolton 1968).

CHAPTER VI

LIFE TABLES AND STABLE POPULATION MODELS

In chapter 4, the available census materials for the Semai were examined and, in chapter 5, the fertility, mortality and population growth rates for the SA area Semai were presented. Given these data, it is possible to construct life tables for the Semai based on stable population methods (U.N. 1967). In this chapter the Semai population will be fitted to one of the family of stable populations produced by Weiss (1973).

A number of procedures exist for choosing the most appropriate stable population (U.N. 1967, Weiss 1973). Since the concern is to provide an estimate of the underlying average rates for a large portion of the Semai (the less acculturated subset of the population), the 1965 Jabatan Orang Asli census for Pahang (N=3810) will be used as the reference population to be compared to the stable models. Unfortunately, no fertility or mortality data exist for this group as a whole. It will be necessary, therefore, to use the SA area data as an approximation to the overall figures.

The age-sex structure of a stable population is determined by both mortality and fertility. If fertility is known, a stable population may be found which provides the appropriate levels of mortality for the observed age-sex structure. Correspondingly, a known level of mortality leads to an appropriate fertility level. In procedural terms, this translates into two suitable fitting methods. On the one hand, a census and a growth rate (fertility minus mortality) may be used to locate the best stable population (i.e., one that duplicates the percentages of individuals in the age categories at that growth rate). Or, an estimate of mortality may be used to identify the model life table, and the growth rate may be ascertained by finding the best fitting stable population associated with that life table.

In the present case, estimates of mortality, fertility and population growth are available. Because they are derived from the SA area population, however, they may not be taken to be the rates necessarily operating in the East Semai as a whole. The strategy, then, must be to treat these values *as if* they were representative. If the SA area rates lead to a stable population (age-sex structure) congruent with the East Semai census, this may be taken as evidence for their generality. Insofar as they do not, the SA estimates may be rejected as either inappropriate to the larger population or as misestimates.

In theory, stable population analysis depends upon a history of constant fertility and mortality for at least 100 years. In practice, it is useful whenever fertility and mortality have been subject to only minor fluctuations during the preceding fifty or sixty years (U.N. 1967). Major trends such as those produced when modern medicine is introduced, or a major disease is eradicated, or birth control is adopted, bias the estimates derived from stable population methods.

As has already been discussed, the West Semai population seems an unlikely candidate for stable population analysis. Contact with non-Semai has been heavy and prolonged. The East Semai may be more likely to fulfill the necessary conditions. However, it is difficult to demonstrate this in the absence of several censuses of equal coverage over a reasonably long time period. The census material which is available has been discussed in chapter 4. There it was pointed out that there was no regular trend apparent in the SA area. The absence of birth control methods and the absence of a perceptible pattern of change in marriage age as evidenced by genealogies, suggests that fertility may not have changed markedly over the last several generations. As East Semai become less reluctant to accept medical treatment, mortality may diminish. At present, however, the assumption of relative stability does not seem unwarranted.

As previously noted (chapter 4), the 1965 census is undoubtedly characterized by a pattern of gross age misestimation. The Semai census is not unique in this respect. Indeed, the problem is widespread in many national censuses. A particular pattern found extensively in African and South Asian female censuses (U.N. 1967) shows a marked surplus at ages five to nine, a deficit in the adolescent ages (10-19) and a surplus in the principal reproductive ages (25-34). This pattern has been shown to occur in all of the

LIFE TABLES AND STABLE POPULATION MODELS 73

countries of sub-Saharan Africa, as well as in Indonesia, India, and Pakistan (although not in Malaya). The common feature of all these censuses is that individuals' ages are assigned by the census-taker. This suggests that there is a similar tendency among census-takers to estimate the ages of females by life-events, especially marriage and childbirth (see U.N. 1967 for a detailed discussion of these points). The male age distributions in these countries show a much less uniform pattern of misestimation. Moreover, the distortion may be (and probably is) as large as in the female distribution. Where a pattern exists, it may be compensated for. Where there is no pattern, this is impossible. Thus, if a female population may be shown to follow the African-South Asian distribution, the female age distribution is the better choice for estimating population characteristics (U.N. 1967).

The East Semai female population may be examined for conformity with the African-South Asian pattern following the procedure suggested by the U.N. Manual ("Methods of Estimating Basic Demographic Measures from Incomplete Data"). First, a model stable population with the same proportion of the female population younger than age thirty-five and with an expectation of life at birth (e_0) of forty years is chosen.[1] In the Semai case, this corresponds to mortality level nine with growth rate of 20.0 in the Coale and Demeny (1966) West family of model stable populations. The ogives (cumulative proportions of the population under a certain age) of the Semai female population are then compared to the model, C_5-C_5 stable (proportion under age five in the Semai population, C_5, minus the corresponding figure in the stable population, C_5 stable) through C_{40}.

Figure 6.1 illustrates the results of this procedure (and may be compared to those in Figure 10, U.N. 1967). The pattern appears to be identical to the twenty-nine cases examined by the writers of the U.N. Manual. That is, "(1) the cumulative age distribution rises (relative to the stable) from age 5 to 10; (2) it falls from age 10 to 15 and from 15 to 20; (3) it rises from 25 to 30, and from 30 to 35." It may be concluded that the Semai female census follows the typical African-South Asian pattern of age misestimation. This is not surprising since few if any East

---

[1] The choice of e_0=40 is arbitrary (U.N. 1967) and does not affect the elucidation of the pattern of age misestimation.

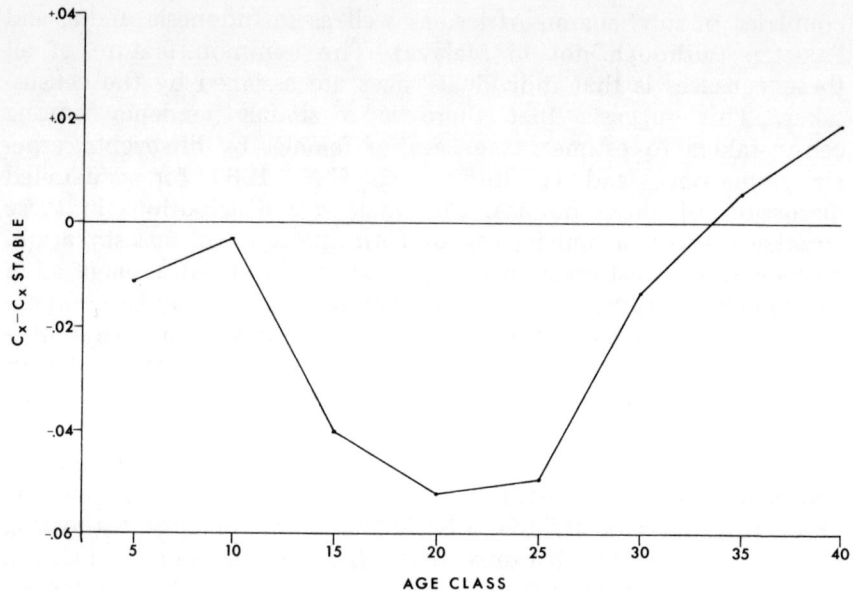

Fig. 6.1 Comparison of female cumulative age distribution (C_x) of the 1965 Pahang census (unsmoothed) with Coale and Demeny (1966) model distribution having $e_0=30$ and $r=0.020$.

Semai know their own ages, and ages were almost certainly assigned by (Malay) census-takers.

Having demonstrated this pattern, it follows that the female age distribution should be used in comparison with the model tables (assuming that the Semai census is similar to the others in showing greater and less regular distortion in the male age estimates). It remains to fit this age distribution to a stable population model taking into account the pattern of age-misestimation.

The procedure advocated by the U.N. Manual (1967) under these circumstances assumes that a reliable estimate of the growth rate is known. As has been shown (chapter 5), the growth rate for the SA area probably lies within the range 0.007 to 0.010. It was noted, however, that these figures are uncertain due to the difficulty of factoring out the effects of migration. Also, two censuses for the East Semai population as a whole are not available which means that an intercensal rate of increase for the entire group may not be calculated.

For these reasons, the East Semai female age distribution will be compared to a broad spectrum of stable models across a wide range of growth rates. The set of models which best fit the female age distribution will then be evaluated for their correspondence with fertility and mortality rates to achieve the best fit to the whole set of parameters (see also Neel and Weiss 1975). It may be expected that the growth rate found to be the best fit should be close to the SA area values. However, the use of many comparison growth models will allow this parameter to be assessed.

The model age distributions chosen for the analysis were derived from the seventy-two stationary (zero growth) model life tables constructed by Weiss (1973) from data on anthropological populations. In addition, the series of West Model Tables of Coale and Demeny (1966) were also compared to the Semai data.

Weiss' model life tables associate a series of nine juvenile mortality rates (varying from a survivorship at age fifteen of 30 percent to 70 percent) with eight adult mortality schedules (varying from an expectation of life at age fifteen from fifteen to thirty years). In contrast to the series of combinations of infant and juvenile mortality in the Weiss tables, the Coale and Demeny tables relate juvenile and adult mortality according to the observed pattern in a variety of well-studied national populations. Since it is not necessarily the case that populations such as the Semai would conform to this pattern, the Weiss tables were chosen.

The procedure of Neel and Weiss (1975) was followed in comparing the East Semai female census population to the Weiss stable population models. Weiss' stationary models were transformed to reflect a series of growth rates ranging from 0.1 percent to 2.0 per year (in 0.1 percent steps to 1.0 percent; then at 1.2 percent, 1.5 percent, 1.8 percent and 2.0 percent). Seventy-two families of tables were generated, each family determined by the underlying model life table (mortality rates) and each member of the family differing by the amount of growth per annum. In all, 1,080 model tables (fifteen growth rates times seventy-two model tables) were examined for fit.

For each model stable population, the average fertility rate, $\bar{f}$, was determined (Weiss 1973). That is, the rate which would satisfy the basic equation of the stable population

$$1 = e^{-r\bar{x}} L_x K_x \bar{f}$$

where x is the age class, $\bar{x}$ the midpoint of an age class, L_x the sum of survivorships for age class x taken from Weiss' model life table, and K_x the age-specific fertility rates derived from the SA area population (see chapter 5). The value of $\bar{f}$ varies for each model stable population depending on the growth rate and mortality. It allows a connection to be made between the fertility rates implied by the model and the empirical rates derived from the population through the relative fertility rates, K_x. The product of K_x and $\bar{f}$ should equal the empirical rate for age class x.

The birth rate in the model population may also be calculated as $b=1/L_x e^{-r\bar{x}}$; the death rate, d, is then simply the difference between the birth and growth rates (d=b-r). The percentage distribution of the model populations by age classes is:

$$c_x e = bL_x e^{-r\bar{x}}$$

A variety of other measures were also calculated for each model population including the dependency ratio (the proportion of the populations who are dependent on the economically productive proportion, $c_{0-15} + c_{55-80}/c_{20-50}$), and the average age of the population (the midpoint of each age class, $\bar{x}$, multiplied by the proportion within the class, c_x). The ogives (C_x) of the age distribution were also computed as a cumulation of the age class percentages.

Thus, a variety of model parameters are available for comparison with the empirical population: the model age distribution, the average fertility rate, the crude birth and death rates, and the growth rate. As Neel and Weiss (1975) point out, however, no single quantitative criterion exists for guaranteeing which model table is the *true* one. Their procedure (and the one to be employed in this work) was to choose male and female model life tables which satisfied a variety of criteria including:

(1) equivalent growth rates for both sexes (clearly, if growth were differential over any length of time, one sex would replace the other, an impossible situation)
(2) Good correspondence between the age distributions of the model and the empirical populations
(3) Good correspondence between fertility rates of the model and empirical populations
(4) General consistency in the other features of the population (e.g., sex ratio)

LIFE TABLES AND STABLE POPULATION MODELS 77

At the same time, the goal of the modeling should not be forgotten. The method is not directed at simply fitting the empirical data. If this were the only object, the analysis would be redundant. The interest of the model is in tying together a variety of observations into a consistent picture of the average underlying rates operating in the East Semai population. By varying the mortality and growth rates it is possible to arrive at a (potentially infinite) set of model populations which would have the same age distribution. For example, as Neel and Weiss note, a higher growth rate may be balanced by lower mortality rates to yield the same age distribution as another model with lower growth and higher mortality rates. But, due to the interrelationships of all the parameters, each will be affected by increased (or decreased) mortality or growth rates. Therefore, the *overall* consistency of model and real populations is of prime importance. Moreover, when the "real" data appear to be inconsistent with respect to each other, the models may give a better representation of the true rates than the empirical data (particularly for populations such as the Semai in which the data base is not large and problems of misestimation are likely).

Returning to the actual comparison, the quality of fit of the age distributions was evaluated by the ogives, C_x, rather than age class percentages, c_x. This allows the effect of the demonstrated age misestimation in the East Semai female population to be taken into account. According to the U.N. Manual (1967), values associated with C_{35} and C_{10} are expected to be at the correct level for populations exhibiting the African-South Asian type of age misestimation. Since the East Semai female population follows this pattern, the comparison will be primarily concerned with these ogives.

Not surprisingly, several model age distributions are in reasonable correspondence with the observed distributions at C_{10} and C_{35}. The best fitting model table at C_{35} is Weiss' (1973) MT: 27.5-50[2] at R=0.003 (the difference between the real and model is negligible, $\triangle$ =.0001). However, the fit with estimated fertility, birth and death rates is not so good.

The best *overall* fit occurs with MT: 30-60 at a growth rate of 0.7 percent. Figure 6.2 shows the comparison between the stable

---

[2]In Weiss' notation, MT: *i-j* refers to a model table with adult mortality level *i* and juvenile mortality level *j*; e.g., MT: 27.5-50 refers to that table with e_{15} of 27.5 years and l_{15} of 50.

78 THE DEMOGRAPHY OF THE SEMAI SENOI

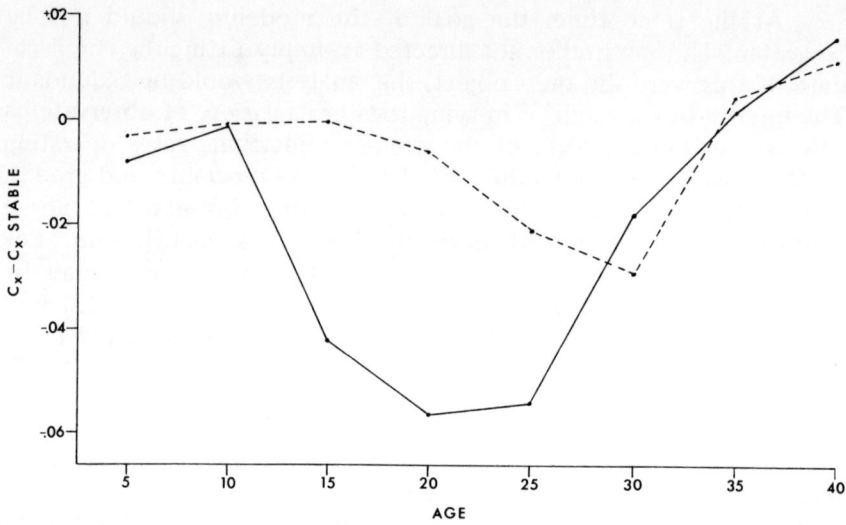

Fig. 6.2 Comparison of female cumulative age distribution (C_x) with the best-fitting model distribution from Weiss (1973) The solid line represents the 1965 Pahang census; the dashed line the SA area distribution.

and census ogives for both the total East Semai females and for the females given ages by the author in the SA area. The shape of the East Semai female curve closely resembles that in Figure 6.1 based on the Coale and Demeny tables, illustrating the basic similarity between the Coale and Demeny and Weiss tables. The SA area females curve demonstrates my slightly different pattern of age misestimation. Agreement is good through age 20 and at C_{35} suggesting a tendency on my part to underestimate ages of some women in the later childbearing ages (though never enough to affect the cumulative age percentages by more than 3 percent). Despite the apparent age misestimation, the index of dissimilarity ($\triangle$, the sum of the absolute values of the difference between the model and census populations over all age classes) is only 0.134, almost identical to the value obtained by Neel and Weiss (1975) for Yanomama Indian females ($\triangle$ =0.13). The appropriate life table (from Weiss 1973) along with age distribution, c_x, for the females is given in Table 6.1. Before examining the fit of the female parameters to the Semai, the male table will be chosen. Remembering that in African-South Asian type populations the age distortion

LIFE TABLES AND STABLE POPULATION MODELS

TABLE 6.1
EAST SEMAI FEMALE MODEL LIFE TABLE

Ages	$_nq_x$	l_x	$_nL_x$	T_x	e_x	c_x
0	0.2000	100.0	87.	2827.	28.3	3.7
1	0.1200	80.0	295.	2740.	34.3	12.2
5	0.0910	70.4	336.	2446.	34.7	13.4
10	0.0624	64.0	310.	2110.	33.0	12.0
15	0.1154	60.0	282.	1800.	30.0	10.5
20	0.1178	53.1	249.	1517.	28.6	9.0
25	0.1203	46.8	220.	1268.	27.1	7.6
30	0.1228	41.2	193.	1048.	25.4	6.5
35	0.1254	36.1	169.	855.	23.7	5.5
40	0.1280	31.6	148.	686.	21.7	4.6
45	0.1306	27.6	129.	538.	19.5	3.9
50	0.1334	24.0	112.	410.	17.1	3.3
55	0.1663	20.8	95.	298.	14.3	2.7
60	0.2251	17.3	77.	203.	11.7	2.1
65	0.2974	13.4	57.	126.	9.4	1.5
70	0.3986	9.4	38.	69.	7.3	1.0
75	0.5336	5.7	21.	31.	5.5	0.5
80	1.0000	2.6	10.	10.	3.9	0.2

NOTE: From Weiss (1973). The column headings are, with the addition of the age composition, the standard ones of the life table (see Weiss or Barclay 1958). That is, column 1, the age at the beginning of the class; $_nq_x$, the probability of dying between x and x+n; l_x, the number of survivors from an initial population of 100; $_nL_x$, the number of years lived by the persons between age x and age x+n; T_x, the sum of person-years lived by the cohort to age x; e_x, the life expectancy; and, c_x, the proportion of the population in the age class.

in the male census is likely to be more pronounced than in the female, an excellent fit to the East Semai male census figures is not to be expected. However, assuming that the female fit is reasonably accurate, a further constraint is placed on the male life table. That is, the pattern of male mortality when considered with that of the females should produce the observed sex ratios throughout the age classes. The degree to which this occurs will provide another check on the overall consistency of the models. Moreover, as stated above, the fitting criteria require that the growth rate of the male population should equal that of the female (i.e., r = 0.7%).

The male life table which most satisfactorily fits these criteria is Weiss' MT: 35-60. Figure 6.3 shows the correspondence for males in a similar manner to Fig. 6.2 for females. The curve resembles the female pattern by sinking sharply in the 15 to 25

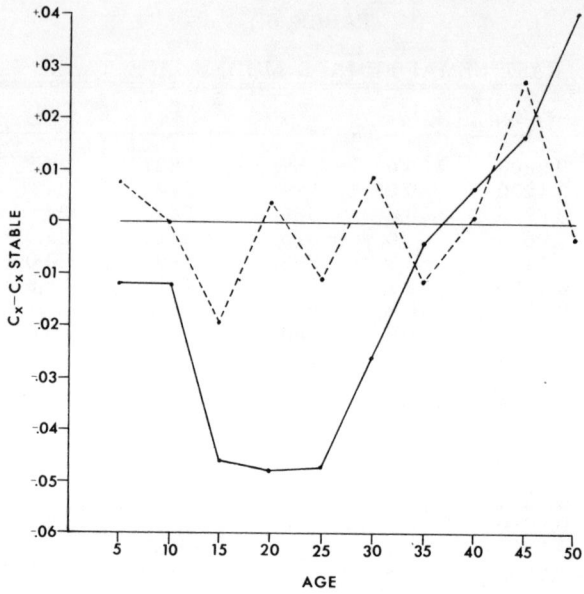

Fig. 6.3 Comparison of male cumulative age distribution (C_x) with the best-fitting model distribution from Weiss (1973). The solid line represents the 1965 Pahang census; the dashed line, SA settlement.

year age range and fitting well at C_{35}. Also shown is the curve of differences in ogives between the male population of SA settlement (N=156) and the model. Considerable effort was expended over a several month period to obtain accurate ages from these men. Given the very small size of the sample, it is interesting that the curve oscillates with reasonably low amplitude around a mean difference of 0 thus increasing confidence in the general fit to the model. The appropriate life table (again from Weiss 1973) is given in Table 6.2.

The goodness of fit of the model population will now be examined for the other parameters. Although the correspondence in age distribution has been presented first, the actual choice of the male and female models was made on the basis of multiple criteria. The comparisons will necessitate restating some of the measures of fertility and mortality already obtained in chapter 5. Some estimates may be expected to be more accurate than others;

LIFE TABLES AND STABLE POPULATION MODELS

TABLE 6.2
EAST SEMAI MALE MODEL LIFE TABLE

Ages	$_nq_x$	l_x	$_nL_x$	T_x	e_x	c_x
0	0.2000	100.0	87.	3128.	31.3	3.4
1	0.1200	80.0	295.	3041.	38.0	11.2
5	0.0910	70.4	336.	2746.	39.0	12.3
10	0.0624	64.0	310.	2410.	37.7	11.0
15	0.0897	60.0	286.	2100.	35.0	9.8
20	0.0912	54.6	260.	1814.	33.2	8.6
25	0.0927	49.6	237.	1553.	31.3	7.6
30	0.0942	45.0	214.	1317.	29.2	6.6
35	0.0957	40.8	194.	1102.	27.0	5.8
40	0.0972	36.9	175.	908.	24.6	5.0
45	0.0988	33.3	158.	733.	22.0	4.4
50	0.1004	30.0	142.	575.	19.1	3.8
55	0.1311	27.0	126.	432.	16.0	3.3
60	0.1824	23.5	107.	306.	13.0	2.7
65	0.2493	19.2	84.	199.	10.4	2.0
70	0.3450	14.4	60.	116.	8.0	1.4
75	0.4746	9.4	36.	56.	5.9	0.8
80	1.0000	5.0	20.	20.	4.0	0.4

NOTE: See Table 6.1 for explanation of the column headings.

the probable degree of accuracy will be specified in the following discussion.

Looking initially at the age-specific fertility rates, it can be seen in Table 6.3 that the model populations are very close to the calculated rates. The total number of offspring born of women

TABLE 6.3
COMPARISON OF MODEL AND OBSERVED AGE-SPECIFIC FERTILITY RATES

	Age Class					
	15-19	20-24	25-29	30-34	35-39	40-44
Observed	.107	.289	.291	.278	.141	.032
Model	.107	.292	.294	.279	.143	.031

NOTE: Annual rates for male and female offspring combined. Total fertility observed in women greater than forty-five years is 5.69; completed fertility on the model is 5.73.

surviving through the reproductive ages was 5.69 in the SA area sample; the model predicts a completed family size of 5.73.

The mortality rates (q_x) shown in the model life tables appear to be somewhat higher in the juvenile ages and slightly lower in the post-forty year age class than would have been expected from the observed rates in the SA area (see Figure 6.4). However, these rates were based on the small number of deaths which occurred in the SA area (particularly SA settlement) over the last twenty years and therefore may not be expected to be absolutely accurate. It is nonetheless noteworthy that the series of estimates of survivorship

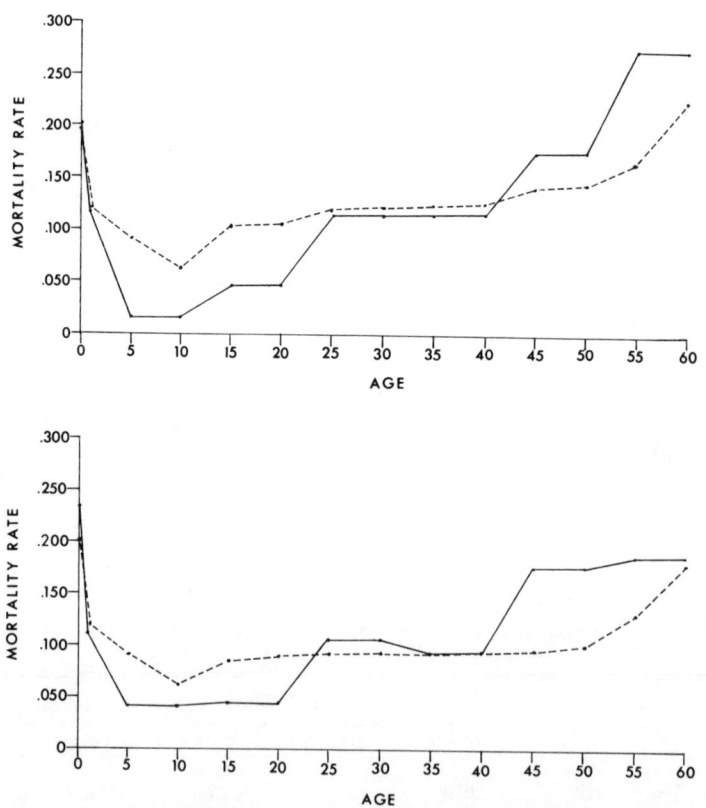

Fig. 6.4 Comparison of empirical and model mortality rates. The solid lines represent the empircal values; dashed lines, the model rates. The upper figure is for females; the lower, males.

LIFE TABLES AND STABLE POPULATION MODELS 83

obtained from female reproductive histories by the Brass method are in close agreement with the model. The estimate of l_2 obtained by the Brass method was 70.3 percent leading to an expected l_{15} of 59 percent to 60 percent. According to the U.N. Manual (1967), l_2 is the best estimate of survivorship obtainable by the Brass method. The actual l_{15} derived from survivorship of children of mothers aged forty to forty-four was 58.5 percent. The model tables provide for 60 percent of persons born surviving to age fifteen (l_{15}).

The discrepancies between the model and empirical rates are to some degree a result of the nature of the fitting process. It would have been a simple matter to choose the table which best matched the empirical age-specific rates. However, as was discussed above, in order to fit the age distribution with a fixed mortality schedule, the growth rate would be determined as well. In addition, the relationship between male and female mortality determines the sex ratio (see below). In order to have fit the census age distribution with a higher mortality model life table in the present case, the growth rate would necessarily have been quite low, on the order of 0.1 percent to 0.3 percent per annum. The other parameters, birth and death rates, would also have been out of line with the empirical estimates.

Indeed, the growth rate actually chosen in the model is lower than predicted from the unadjusted intercensal rates of increase. It does fit the estimate based on the removal of migrants from the census populations. By examining many models at different growth rates, it has been possible to show that the overall Semai intercensal rates of increase and those calculated on the basis of the 1960, 1965, and 1969 SA area censuses must be too high. A rate of growth higher than 0.7 percent would have required mortality rates to be considerably below those estimated from the data. The aim of the analysis was to obtain the best fit to all the data; in this sense the model tables chosen are the optima.

Additional support for the quality of the fit may be obtained from a comparison of observed and expected sex ratios (Neel and Weiss 1975). The overall sex ratio for the East Semai census was 1.193. A definite pattern of increasing sex ratios with age may be seen in these data. The model tables not only reproduce the overall sex ratio (predicted sex ratio on the model is 1.183) but also mirror the trend of increasing masculinity with age.

TABLE 6.4

COMPARISON OF MODEL AND OBSERVED SEX RATIOS

Age Class	Raw Data	Smoothed Data*	Model[+]	Error Ratio[‡]
0- 4	1.065	1.065	1.070	1.005
5- 9	1.041	1.074	1.070	0.996
10-14	1.154	1.133	1.070	0.944
15-19	1.258	1.143	1.085	0.949
20-24	1.125	1.147	1.117	0.974
25-29	1.041	1.126	1.153	1.024
30-34	1.230	1.166	1.186	1.017
35-39	1.202	1.128	1.228	1.008
40-44	0.947	1.212	1.265	1.044
45-49	1.596	1.263	1.311	1.038
50-54	1.446	1.702	1.357	0.797
55-59	3.176	2.172	1.555	0.716

*Smoothed by the method of running averages.
[+]Derived from the life tables by:

sex ratio $sr_x = (1.07)$ male L_x/female L_x

where x is the age class, 1.07 the sex ratio at birth, male L_x the sum of the male survivors in the xth age class, and female L_x the same for females.

[‡]The ratio of the predicted to observed values. The overall error ratio for the age classes under fifty is 1.008.

Due to the errors of age estimation in the census, the data are represented in Figure 6.5 as cumulative ratios (e.g., the sex ratio at age forty represents the total number of males less than age forty divided by the total number of females less than forty). This procedure smooths out some of the irregularities in the data due to age misestimations. The raw data are presented in Table 6.4 along with data smoothed by the method of running averages.

The overall error is low for the ages under fifty years. Most of the discrepancies appear to be due to age misestimation (as suggested by the smoothness of the cumulative distribution in Figure 6.5). The excess of males between the ages of fifteen and thirty in the census population is most likely a result of the characteristic pattern of female age misestimation of the African-South Asian pattern; even if males are also erroneously placed in the older age brackets, the tendency on the part of the census-takers may be more pronounced in the case of the females of this age group.

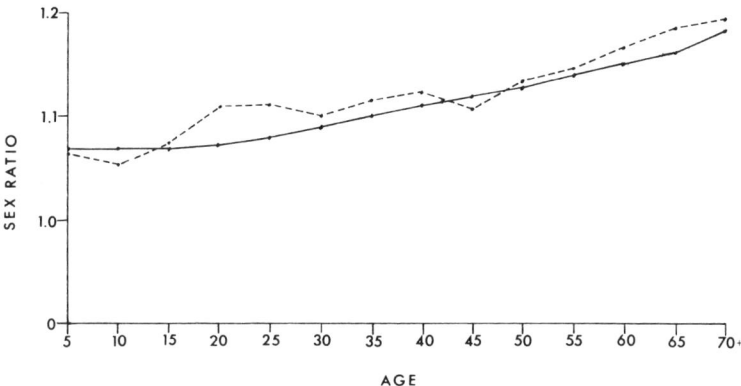

Fig. 6.5 Graph of the sex ratio of the 1965 Pahang census by cumulative age; i.e., sex ratio at age 30 is the total number of males less than age 30 divided by the total number of females less than age 30. The solid line represents the model values; the dashed line, the empirical values.

It should also be noted that the sex ratio at birth is set at 1.07 in these calculations, rather than at the more usual 1.05. The justification for this rests on the discussion in Chapter 4 regarding the sex ratio. It is also true that the sex ratio at birth in the Malay population is high—1,062 male births per 1,000 female births as stated in the report on the 1947 Malayan census (Tufo 1949). If, in fact, the percentage of male births is lower than this, the differential in male/female mortality must be even greater than the present model predicts.

The higher male mortality in the model life tables chosen for the Semai runs counter to the usual expectation in large national populations and, neglecting preferential female infanticide, in anthropological populations as well (e.g., Neel and Weiss 1975). Nonetheless, "it is possible to find many examples of female mortality higher than male mortality" (U.N. 1967). One well-documented case is the population of India (Visaria 1963, cited in U.N. 1967). In the specific case of the Malayan Aborigines, other authors have also suggested that female mortality rates must be higher than those of males (Dentan 1968, Tufo 1949). Alternative explanations of the high sex ratio are possible, e.g., higher secondary sex ratio or a systematic underreporting of females. The first alternative would appear to be even more unlikely than the finding of higher male mortality. The second is possible but unlikely, particularly in the SA area where my long residence involved seeing most members of the population. The pattern of *increasing* masculinity makes preferential female infanticide unlikely since this practice leads to high sex ratios in the younger ages. A regime of declining female infanticide through time could account for the observed sex ratios; however, the sex ratios for the aborigines (including several ethnic groups) in the 1901, and 1911 censuses were, respectively, 1.124 and 1.134 and in 1947, 1.100 (Tufo 1949). The East Semai ratio of 1.193 is thus higher than that obtained during the period in which the hypothetical infanticide must have been practiced. Although declining female infanticide rates may not be totally excluded as a possibility, the differential female mortality predicted by the present model seems more economical. This is particularly true when the high female rate of death in childbirth is considered (see chapter 5).

Thus, the general overall fit of the East Semai data to the model is quite good. This may be summarized in terms of criteria used to establish the fit:
(1) The growth rates for both sexes are the same: 0.7 percent
(2) The fit for both age distributions is good
(3) The fertility rates predicted by the model are very close to those estimated from the data
(4) Other measures are consistent with the model (sex ratio and total fertility)

As Neel and Weiss (1975) caution, this does not necessarily mean that the model rates must be absolutely accurate. Particular local groups might experience deviations from the model (this problem will be explored further in the next chapter). Nevertheless, the claim that the model rates characterize the general level of Semai mortality and fertility seems justified. The models define the central tendency of a region of values within which the Semai rates may be expected to fall.

Having concluded that the model is a reasonable representation of the underlying East Semai demographic structure, it remains to summarize the characteristics of the model. The annual rate of growth is 0.7 percent. Infant mortality is approximately 200 per 1,000 for both males and females with greater female mortality after age 15. Expectation of life at birth (e_0) is 31.3 years for males and 28.3 years for females. This is somewhat higher than the average values cited by Weiss (1973) for "living primitives" (e_0 =21.5), yet is still a good deal lower than is currently true for most national populations (modern Norway having one of the highest e_0 of 76.6 years). The differential mortality of females in the post-fifteen year old age group (e_{15} for males is 35 years; for females, 30 years) leads to a high overall sex ratio (greater than 1.18).

The age composition for males is not markedly young with only 38 percent less than age fifteen. The average age of males is 25.7 years and the dependency ratio is 1.095. The female population is slightly younger with 41 percent less than fifteen years old; the average age is 23.9 and the dependency ratio is 1.102.

The measures calculated for the model population indicate a moderately high level of fertility. The completed family size of women surviving past menopause is 5.73. Only 40 percent of women reaching age fifteen will survive through the reproductive period (l_{50}/l_{15}); the mean number of live births to women reaching at least age fifteen is approximately 4.17. Fertility begins at a relatively early age; the mean age of the fertility schedule is 28.5 years. The net reproduction rate (R_0) is 1.21 and the gross reproductive rate is 2.77. The generation length (the time it would take for a cohort of women to increase themselves R_0 times) is 27.2 years. The average woman in the fertile age classes will give birth to 0.2 children annually (calculated from the fertility schedule weighted by the percentages in the age classes); that is, one offspring will be produced every five years on the average.

The crude birth rate of the female model population is 0.042 and 0.039 for males (due to the excess of males in the population). It may be noted parenthetically that this measure also supports the choice of the male model life table. After fitting the females to the model, it was possible to calculate the expected male birth rate as follows:

$$\text{Male birth rate} = \text{Female birth rate} \times \frac{\text{sex ratio at birth}}{\text{sex ratio in the population}}$$

(U.N. 1967). The predicted male birth rate from this calculation was 0.038; the birth rate of the male model table chosen was in close agreement (0.039). The combined crude birth rate for the total population (male and female) is 0.040; the overall crude death rate (CBR-r) is thus 0.033.

TABLE 6.5
COMPARISON OF SEMAI MODEL RATES TO OTHER POPULATIONS (FEMALE)

Population	Crude Birth Rate	Crude Death Rate	R	TFF	GRR	NRR	Sex Ratio at Birth	Generation Length
Semai	.042	.035	.007	5.73	2.77	1.21	1.07	27.23
Yanomama	.059	.050	.009	8.20	3.90	1.25	1.05	26.60
Malaysia, 1969	.039	.008	.031	5.92	2.89	2.52	1.05	27.94
Madagascar, 1966	.044	.025	.019	6.77	3.29	1.88	1.06	27.91
United States, 1966	.018	.010	.008	2.74	1.34	1.29	1.05	26.17
Norway, 1967	.017	.009	.008	2.80	1.36	1.33	1.06	27.25

SOURCES: The Yanomama figures are from Neel and Weiss (1975). The figures for the national populations are from Keyfitz and Fleiger (1971).

NOTE: The rates for Madagascar are representative of a relatively high mortality population by national standards; those for the United States and Norway represent low mortality populations.

LIFE TABLES AND STABLE POPULATION MODELS

In order to provide some perspective, the Semai rates are compared to several national populations (from Keyfitz and Flieger 1971) and another anthropological population (Neel and Weiss 1975) in Table 6.5. Further comparative data are available in Keyfitz and Flieger (1971) and Weiss (1973).

Several aspects of Semai demographic structure are notable in this comparison. In terms of birth rates, the Semai values are bracketed by the underdeveloped countries of Malaysia and Madagascar, are considerably lower than those for the Yanomama, and considerably higher than those for the developed countries. The Semai crude death rate, however, is higher than any other population excepting the Yanomama. This results in a crude rate of increase comparable to the United States and Norway. In keeping with the similar crude birth rates, the other measures of fertility (TFF, GRR, NRR) are in line with the underdeveloped countries. The mean generation length is remarkably similar across the whole range of populations.

In this chapter, the census age distributions have been fit by model life tables with a reasonable degree of confidence. A variety of measures of the Semai demographic structure are all consistent with each other and with the model. From the model tables a coherent overall picture of Semai demography has been obtained. Although it must be borne in mind that these rates may differ in small measure from the true rates or the rates at any one time in a subdivision of the population (Neel and Weiss 1975) the model gives a generalized description that is as good as may be expected in the absence of written records and vital registration.

CHAPTER VII

SIMULATION

In recent years, a variety of problems have been investigated using Monte Carlo simulation methods (for a review and examples see MacCluer 1973 and Dyke and MacCluer 1974). Two features of anthropological populations make simulation a useful tool in the study of their demography. In the first place, most populations studied by anthropologists are small; even if the tribe or ethnic group is large, the intensive methods used by anthropologists usually preclude the study of populations which are large by demographer's standards.

Secondly, the data collected by retrospective methods or by short-term observation are often uncertain and inaccurate in comparison with data from vital registries or written records. As was outlined in chapter 6, one way to deal with these problems is to fit a stable population model to the data and ascribe the characteristics of the model to the population. Alternatively, the rates can be estimated by simulation (Dyke and MacCluer 1973).

The advantage of using Monte Carlo simulation (as opposed to deterministic models) is that an idea of the variation in basic parameters through time or in different geographic subdivisions of the population may be gained. Although the stable population model may be accepted as a good representation of the population as a whole, it might be asked, how much chance difference in population composition or crude birth rate might be expected within a subdivision of the East Semai or within one settlement through time assuming that the overall fertility and mortality rates do not vary.

This question has some practical significance since anthropologists may find themselves with a population of only a few hundred individuals. Following Weiss' (1973) advice, they may attempt to fit these data to a stable model. If random variation is large, the model may bear little resemblance to the true rates operative in the population. For instance, in one case, Weiss suggests fitting a model on the basis of C_{15} (the proportion of the population under fifteen years of age) and the crude death rate. If no other data are available, this procedure might be better than nothing, and for some questions it may be sufficient. Nonetheless, it would be useful to know how much variation to expect in these rates and percentages. Clearly, if the crude death rate may vary between ten and fifty due to chance fluctuations in a small population, it may not be a very reliable indicator of the total demographic structure.

Attempts have been made to derive analytic solutions for the variances of demographic characteristics (Keyfitz 1968). However, the assumptions seem restrictive and the methods difficult to apply in practice.

In a simulation the degree of variation in various rates and ratios using an invariant mortality and fertility schedule may be assessed. That is, with the model age-specific fertilities and male and female life tables as input, it is possible to observe the chance fluctuations from year to year in the population composition, crude birth and death rates, and other characteristics of interest. This procedure can also determine which rates are more variable (MacCluer 1973).

A further advantage of simulation is that it makes possible detailed examination of some effects of real populations which are not accounted for in stable population models. For example, real populations have mating rules. In so far as these rules affect the probability of persons remaining unmarried and childless, these rules may result in lower growth rates than might be predicted from the stable population model.

These applications and others are reviewed in detail by MacCluer (1973). Rather than provide further abstract examples of its potential, I will show how Monte Carlo simulation can supplement the stable population analysis of the Semai population.

The Program

Betsy Dickinson Fix and I have written a Monte Carlo simulation program in FORTRAN IV which has been used in

SIMULATION

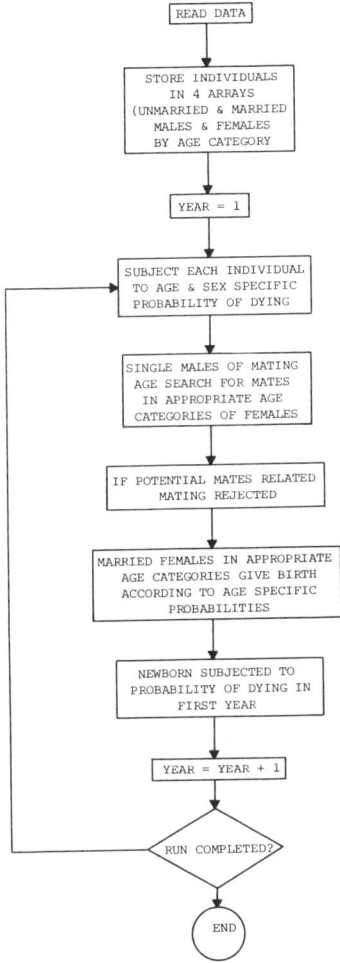

Fig. 7.1 Simplified flow chart of the simulation program.

measuring potential endogamy in small populations (Fix 1973). The program is designed to mimic the basic demographic processes of a real population including the cycles of birth, mating, reproduction, and death. Table 7.1 lists the input information for each individual in the population and the rates (probabilities) at which the vital events occur in the population. Table 7.2 shows the output information. Figure 7.1 shows a simplified flow chart of the program.

TABLE 7.1

SIMULATION INPUT

Information on Each Individual	Vital Rates
Sex	Probabilities of:
Age	Male Birth
Unique I.D. No.	Dying (males and females)
Mate's I.D. No.	Reproducing (females 15-44)
Known Ancestor's I.D. Nos. (parents through great-grandparents)	

TABLE 7.2

SIMULATION OUTPUT

Information Printed Every Year:
    Matings rejected due to close consanguinity
    Consanguineous matings
    Births (sex, survival, mother's and father's I.D.s)

Information Printed Every Five Years:

    Population size
    Sex ratio
    No. of male immigrants
    Deaths by age-sex category
    Crude birth and death rates
    Male and female births
    No. of matings
    Population distribution (age and sex, by nos. and percent)
    Frequency of unmarried males and females

Information Printed at the End of the Run:

    Cumulative (average) sex ratio
    Cumulative population distribution
    Cumulative number of deaths by sex and age

The simulation proceeds from a base population provided as input. The information on each individual in the original population comes from the 1969 census of SA settlement and associated genealogies and reproductive histories. The input rates may be varied on the basis of the problem at hand; these may be either empirical rates, or those of the stable population model, or any others of interest. These rates define the probabilities by which individual members of the population are born, give birth or die. The decision for any individual is based on the standard Monte Carlo method. A random number is generated[1] from a uniform distribution between 0 and 1. This number is then compared to the probability (say) of dying for the age and sex status of the reference individual. If, for example, the probability of dying within that year for the particular person is 0.018, and if the random number were less than or equal to 0.018, the individual would "die" and be removed from the population. Exactly similar procedures obtain for giving birth, and for the sex of the offspring. These, then, are treated as random variables and the stochastic properties of the simulation come from chance fluctuations in these events.

The simulation continues year-by-year, subjecting each individual each year to the probability of dying, and females in the reproductive period to the age-specific probability of giving birth, until the specified number of years has elapsed (usually 100 or 200 years).

In addition, as individuals reach the mating age, males begin to search for mates. Thus, in addition to allowing rates to vary randomly, the simulation involves an additional departure from the stable population analysis. It is possible for individuals not to find suitable mates and thus to remain unmarried for short periods or even for the duration of the reproductive period. Since this possibility exists (and occurs) in the real population, the simulation allows some measure of its effect on population growth and other characteristics.

The procedure for mating is designed to follow the general pattern of Semai culture with regard to age-differentials between spouses and consanguinity (see chapter 3). The program has been run with a stringent incest rule, i.e., potential spouses who were related as second cousins or closer were not allowed to mate (Fix 1973). But for the purposes of this work, a looser rule was adopted which allows second cousin mating but not closer. It may be remembered that Semai ideology bars *all* relatives from marrying while, in fact, some relatives do mate and produce offspring.

---

[1]We used the FORTRAN subroutine RANDU with a cycle length of 2^{29} on the UCR IBM 360/50 computer.

The actual method of mate choice in the simulation was for males to seek for a mate among the unmarried females. A male ego of marriageable age searched first among the unmarried females in his own age class, then one category below, one above, two below, three below, and so on until the lower limit of female mating age was reached. Each male searched until mated or until the list of his potential mates was exhausted. If a male encountered a female of the appropriate age, the list of their respective ancestors was compared. If they shared a common ancestor at the grand-parental level or closer, this was recorded and the mating was rejected. Those potential spouses sharing a common great-grandparent were allowed to mate although this relationship was also recorded as consanguineous mating. Once mated, males did not search for additional spouses since polygyny is quite rare among the Semai. Widows and widowers were allowed to remarry.

A further constraint on mating in the artificial population is that the population is closed to migration. Males may search for mates only among those females available as part of their own population. This is patently unreal given the fission-fusion nature of Semai population structure. Migration of individuals, families, and fission groups between local populations is common (see chapter 5). In this sense, then, the model is unreal. However, the portion of the variances of the demographic rates and ratios due exclusively to random fluctuations are not affected. It does mean that any temporal fluctuations in rates recorded in the simulation will be conservative estimates of the actual degree of variation since migration should cause even greater perturbation in population composition than would chance differences in the underlying rates. The simulation thus provides a baseline for gauging variation.

However, if many females were unable to mate and produce offspring, the growth of the population might be strongly biased. In order to avoid this possibility, a provision is made for male migration. The convention adopted is that if the percentage of unmarried females exceeds that in the empirical population (5 percent), the unmarried women are automatically married to a male from an infinite pool of males unrelated to anyone in the population. These males are dummy individuals in that they do not enter the population list but are only added to the card image of the female as her husband. The woman then may reproduce. A catalog of the migrant males and their offspring is kept in order to gauge the impact of migration on the population. The necessity for such males is rare in runs of the larger populations.

Simulation Results

One of the thorniest problems of Monte Carlo simulation lies in verifying whether the program is accurately reproducing the population of interest. Due to the complexity of the program, the fact that the values of many of the demographic characteristics are functions of several input parameters, and that stochastic fluctuations occur, care must be used in evaluating the results. The validation of the program is somewhat simplified in the present case, since the expected values for many of the demographic characteristics are known from the stable population model. For example, the average crude birth rate in the simulated populations should equal approximately 40 per 1,000, the model population value. In contrast, if the field-estimated rates were used, the internal consistency of the parameters could not be assessed. The stable model, by guaranteeing internal consistency and defining the expected values of the parameters, allows the degree of fit of the artificial population to be estimated.

Still, some characteristics will be better tests of goodness of fit than others. Those parameters which are most variable will be least useful in evaluating the logic and functioning of the program. Because the characteristics of the simulated population result from the action of a fixed mortality and fertility schedule, the variation in rates should be greatest in those parameters which are most indirectly related to these schedules and which are based on the fewest number of events. For example, the variation in mean age at paternity might be expected to be large since this is not directly specified as a probability in the program (see also MacCluer, et al. 1971). Mean maternal age should show less variation since it is closely related to probabilities specified as part of the input, i.e., the age-specific probabilities of reproducing. Likewise, the variation in proportions dying within one age category over a five year period might be great even though it is a function of the input age-specific death probabilities since few individuals would die in a short time span. These a priori expectations of stability of parameters do not lead to quantitative statements of the degree of variation. They do, however, provide a guide in the selection of those characteristics to be used to validate the computer model, that is, to verify that the program is correctly simulating the population. Once it is established that the program does not simply generate artifacts of faulty programming, it will be possible to examine the range of variation of particular parameters.

The strategy, then, will be to examine the values of those characteristics which (1) are given by the stable model population, (2) result directly from the operation of the input probabilities, (3) are based on a very large number of events. Not all of these criteria are met for some of the characteristics to be examined, but in combination, several provide a sufficient test of the program. The validation is based on five runs of the program each beginning with different index value for the RANDU subroutine. One of the replicates was run for 100 years, the other four for 200 years.

It may be recalled that the input information consisted of the catalogue of individuals in the SA settlement population (age-sex structure) and the probabilities derived from the model population of sex at birth, age-specific death, and age-specific reproduction (see Table 7.1). The initial age-sex structure was *not* that of the model population; therefore, characteristics dependent on that structure (e.g., birth rate, death rate, proportions dying by age category) will not be equivalent to the model values. However, two characteristics are independent of the age-sex composition of the population: sex ratio at birth and the infant death rate. Once a birth occurs in the artificial populations, the probability that it is male or female and that it lives or dies is independent of every other characteristic of the population and depends only on the probabilities specified as input. Differences from the input values should be due only to random variation. Since the number of births in the five runs made was large, the values should be close and, indeed, they are. The infant death rate was specified by the model life table as 200 per 1,000 for both male and females; the value obtained in the artificial population was 196 per 1,000. Correspondingly, the model sex ratio at birth was 1.070; that in the artificial population was 1.068. In these respects, the program appears to be functioning as designed.

Although the age-specific probabilities of death are provided initially in the program, the number of deaths in any particular category will be relatively low. Of particular importance, however, is the survival of women through the reproductive period (i.e., from ages fifteen to forty-five). By counting all the women reaching age fifteen, a large number of events may be summarized which reflect the effect of the input death rates. According to the model life table, survival of women from age fifteen to age forty-five is 46.0 percent (l_{45}/l_{15}). In the artificial populations, the mean proportion surviving is quite close to this expectation, 46.3 percent.

A further check on the operation of the program which summarizes a variety of specific parameters is the age composition of the total population. For any particular time point in the artificial population, the age structure will not necessarily match the model population due to the smallness of the population (see below for further discussion). However, since the population is censused every five years during the run (i.e., the population composition is computed and printed), a composite total population may be constructed by totaling each census. Each individual will be counted several times during his or her lifetime up to a maximum of thirteen times for those surviving to age sixty-five. The total population for a 200 year run may thus become quite large (as many as 20,000 individuals). With such a large population, random variation should be minimized.

Using this procedure, a close match is obtained between the compositions of the model and artificial populations. The index of dissimilarity, $\triangle$, is less than 0.10 for each comparison. Table 7.3 shows the comparison for the run with the median delta values for males and females.

An obvious discrepancy between the model and artificial populations exists in that individuals in the simulated populations all die before reaching age 70 (to conserve computer memory space requirements), whereas the model population contains individuals surviving to age 80. Almost one half of the $\triangle$ value of 0.095 (0.045) for males is due to this fact. This is also true for the females. If the model population is reduced by removing those aged greater than sixty-five, the comparison yields a $\triangle$ of 0.030 for males and 0.022 for females. When, in addition, it is remembered that the initial population for the simulation was one settlement which did not possess the stable model population structure, the small delta values suggest that the simulation is mimicking the model fertility and mortality rates quite well.

Female reproduction also shows a close agreement between the model and artificial populations. Family sizes were calculated

TABLE 7.3

COMPARISON OF MODEL AND CUMULATIVE ARTIFICIAL POPULATION COMPOSITION

	Males		Females	
	Model c_x	Artificial c_x	Model c_x	Artificial c_x
5	.146	.142	.159	.155
10	.123	.126	.134	.136
15	.110	.115	.120	.125
20	.098	.103	.105	.108
25	.086	.091	.090	.093
30	.076	.079	.076	.081
35	.066	.071	.065	.068
40	.058	.062	.055	.057
45	.050	.056	.046	.049
50	.044	.048	.039	.043
55	.038	.041	.033	.035
60	.033	.037	.027	.028
65	.027	.029	.021	.023
80*	.045	0.000	.030	0.000

*The model population extends to age eighty; all individuals in the artificial population die before reaching age seventy. The total index of dissimilarity for males is 0.098 with the average delta to age sixty-five being 0.004; the total delta for females is 0.070 with the average to age sixty-five being 0.003.

for 1,535 women reaching age fifteen in three runs.[2] The completed family size predicted by the model is 5.73 offspring; the mean number of offspring born to women surviving to age forty-five was 5.72 in the artificial populations. The number of livebirths for all women reaching age fifteen but not necessarily surviving to age forty-five is 4.17 in both the model and artificial populations.

These results may be used to make a methodological point. In order to achieve the model family size, women must be married for their total reproductive life span since marriage is a prerequisite for reproduction in the simulation. This has to some extent been guaranteed in the present simulation program by providing migrant males for unmarried females (see above). Moreover, the design of the program is such that deaths occur first, then matings, and then

---

[2] Since this is a costly procedure, it was not done for all the runs.

reproduction (see the flow chart, Fig. 7.1). Women whose husbands die in the artificial population do not lose time at maternity risk searching for a new mate in this scheme. In a real population, spouse's death and remarriage would not be during a break from reproductive risk. Using the model fertility schedule in a simulation program of greater realism should result in lower than expected family sizes due to periods when the females were unmarried. Because the fertility schedule derived from the empirical population includes these periods of infertility (as well as the presence of sterile women), the sequential nature of the present program produces family sizes which agree with the stable model. If a more realistic program had been employed, the fertility rates would have had to be adjusted to reflect the periods during which females were unmarried and, therefore, not capable of reproducing. Otherwise, the simulated family sizes would have been too low.

Thus, the agreement between the artificial and model populations on several measures leads to a reasonable degree of confidence in the validity of the simulation. Where agreement does not exist, we may search for explanations along two lines: 1) the number of events is so small that random variation masks underlying correspondence, and/or 2) some feature of the simulated population is not present in the model stable population.

An example of the first might be the ten year age class death rates. Only a relatively few individuals will die in a ten year period and, in addition, the age structure may not be in the stable composition. Since both of these factors (number of deaths and number of individuals in the age class) enter into the calculation of the rate, it would hardly be expected that the death rate for any short period of the run would match the model.

The second category of deviation-producing factors might be illustrated by the crude birth and death rates. These rates are somewhat higher in the artificial population than in the model stable population (see Table 7.4). These differences are explicable on the basis of the convention in the simulated population of terminating individuals at age sixty-five. Reference to Table 7.3 will show that the model population contains 4.5 percent more males and 3.0 percent more females than the artificial population (i.e., those in the model population aged sixty-five to eighty). For purposes of illustration, assume that the population size was 100 individuals in the artificial population. In order to obtain a crude birth rate of 0.043 and a crude

TABLE 7.4

COMPARISON OF CRUDE VITAL RATES OF THE MODEL AND ARTIFICIAL POPULATIONS

	Model Population	Artificial Population*
Crude Birth Rate	0.040	0.043
Crude Death Rate	.033	.035
Crude Rate of Natural Increase	.007	.007

*Means of one 100 year run and four 200 year runs.

death rate of 0.035, 4.3 births and 3.5 deaths need to occur during the year. Now assume that individuals in the artificial population may survive to age eighty at the same rate as the model stable population allows. If so, the base population would be increased by 7.5 percent or 7.5 individuals in the illustrative population. The crude birth and death rates calculated on this adjusted base population would become:

Crude Birth Rate: 4.3/107.5 = 0.040
Crude Death Rate: 3.5/107.5 = 0.033

which are exactly the rates predicted by the model. Clearly, lack of correspondence in this case was only due to an artifact of the program. Since this was discovered during the analysis phase of the research, only after the runs were completed, and since individuals greater than age sixty-five would be few and would not be reproducing, and their removal from the artificial population has little effect other than marginally influencing the values of the rates, it was felt to be unnecessary to rerun all the replicates to correct for it.

The mean overall growth rate (calculated as the natural logarithm of the final population size over the initial size divided by the years elapsed, $r=(\ln(N_T/N_0))T)$ is somewhat lower than predicted. According to the model population, $r=0.007$; the mean of the artificial populations was 0.0066. Inclusion of the age bracket sixty-five to eighty leads to a mean growth rate of 0.0069, which is quite close to the expected.

Having demonstrated that the simulation is a valid representation of the population, it is possible to proceed to explore the problem of variation of vital rates in the runs. Although a discrepancy exists in that the oldest members of the artificial populations do not survive, this will have no effect on the study of the degree of *variation* in rates. The actual values of crude rates will be slightly higher than the true rates (and the growth rate will be slightly lower). However, this may easily be taken into account in the analysis.

Variation in Vital Rates

As has been repeatedly noted, a major problem in anthropological demography has been the collection of good quality data on large populations. It will almost always be true that anthropologists will be working with relatively small populations and for a relatively short period of time. This problem is well known and need not be belabored. However, the amount of variation to be expected in these small populations has seldom been dealt with.

Simulation experiments may provide some idea of expected variability. They possess the disadvantage of lack of generality. This will be apparent in the material which follows. Still, for the purposes of the present work, the simulated populations will allow a measure of the degree of deviation from the model population rates which might be found in subpopulations of the East Semai and within such populations through time. In so far as the Semai are representative of small anthropological populations, an idea may be gained regarding the amount of differences from the underlying stable parameters which might be encountered in a study population.

For some measures, variances may be calculated analytically. For example, sex ratio at birth follows a binomial distribution (Visaria 1967). Given the number of births and the probability of a male birth, one may calculate the expected range of the sex ratio at birth among a group of same-sized populations or, correspondingly, the probability that one might find a sex ratio at birth in a subpopulation departing from the true value by a particular amount.

Similarly, death rates are binomially distributed. If the probability of dying before reaching age 1 ($_1q_0$) is taken as q, the probability of surviving as p, and the number of births, N, the variance of q should be pq/N. For the SA area, $_1q_0$ was based on ninety births. The variance from the stable population value (0.2) would thus be 0.00178 yielding a 95 percent confidence interval of

0.116 to 0.284. Reference to Table 5.10 shows that $_1q_0$ estimates for both males and females based on the empirical data fall within this range (males, 0.235; females, 0.197).

Given a known distribution for the infant death rate, simulation does not substantially contribute to our knowledge of variation for this measure. It is nonetheless encouraging that the range observed in the artificial populations follows expectation. The rates were calculated in such a way that the range in number of births in the time interval was between approximately 100 and 200. This involved calculating rates for the first 100 years of the runs of a ten year basis and thereafter on a five year basis: the infant death rates over artificial years 0-10, 10-20, ..., 90-100 were figured along with those of 100-105, ..., 195-200. The mean number of births occurring in the intervals for all runs was 153. A 95 percent confidence interval for N=153 and a mean of 0.2 would be from 0.135 to 0.265. This was almost exactly the range observed in the runs; i.e., from 0.132 to 0.264. This unsurprising result at least suggests that the computer model produces variation in a reasonable manner for an uncomplicated case and therefore may be trusted to generate good estimates for variation for more complicated parameters.

Variations in the age composition of the population is not as obviously related to an underlying distribution. Considerable variation might be expected in small populations and, in fact, may be observed through time in the runs. As shown above, the "mean" composition of the simulated populations is very close to that predicted by the model stable population. However, at any point in artificial time, the composition never exactly matched the stable distribution. The population was censused every five years and the index of dissimilarity, $\Delta = |\Sigma\ c_x - c_x\ \text{stable}|$, was calculated. The mean for the four 200 year runs was 0.192 for the males and 0.173 for the females. Figure 7.2 shows a graph of delta by five year intervals for the artificial population which most closely approached the stable distribution (mean $\Delta = 0.173$) and the most divergent artificial population (mean $\Delta = 0.216$). The population greater than age sixty-five has been excluded from the calculation of delta (see above). Interestingly, for only four time points in the best-fitting run does the delta lie below 0.1, the value which Weiss (1973) suggests as a threshold for a good fit.

According to stable population theory, a population under invariant mortality and fertility schedules should fairly rapidly approach the stable age distribution. After 100 years, the composition should be in a stable configuration whatever its initial distribution might have been. In the present case, the initial population deviated from the stable ($\triangle$ =0.226 for males). A definite movement of the age composition toward the stable may be seen in Figure 7.2; however, even after 200 years the population has still failed to achieve the stable distribution.

A further factor to be considered in evaluating the behavior of the artificial population is that the populations are growing. If, as it appears from the figure, the population composition does not rapidly converge to the stable, a reasonable explanation might be that the numbers of individuals are simply too few to closely match the stable frequencies. A random deviation in numbers of births during one five-year period is enough to distort the composition. The fewer the individuals, the more the apparent random deviation. Thus, in the best-fitting run, the initial number of males was 156 and the final number was 674, showing a more than fourfold increase. For the worst-fitting run, final population size for males was only 471. These figures point to population size as a large factor in determining the closeness of the approach to the stable distribution.

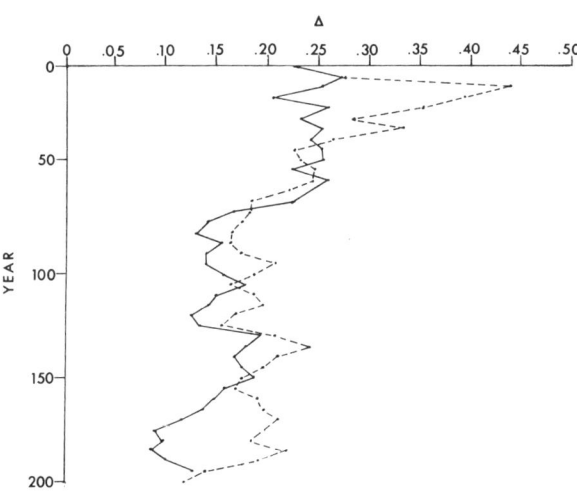

Fig. 7.2 Deviation of the male artificial population composition at five-year intervals from the model stable composition for two runs

It is apparent that even if the total population size exceeds 500 individuals (a reasonably big population by anthropological standards, particularly for hunters and gatherers) and even after 100 years of stable rates, large deviations from the stable composition may be expected. Looking at the last 100 years of the four runs in which both of these conditions are met, a range in delta values from 0.085 to 0.241 was found for the male population and 0.071 to 0.220 for females. The practical implication of this finding is that the age composition of small populations may not be a very sensitive indicator of the underlying vital rates even when stability is assumed and age estimates for the population are accurate. In real populations such as the Semai, it must not be surprising to find even larger deviations. For example even with several thousand individuals in the census, the East Semai population composition does not fit the stable distribution exactly (see chapter 6). Once again, the need for multiple criteria for fitting empirical populations is reinforced.

The crude birth and death rates show a similar wide range of variation. Figure 7.3 presents the distribution of vital rates calculated on the basis of five year's events and on the basis of ten year's events (the inner distribution). The range of values for the crude birth rate is from 25 per 1,000 to 55 per 1,000 based on five year's experience, and from 32 to 52 per 1,000 on the basis of the ten year cumulation. A similar broad interval exists for the crude death rate. The crude rate of natural increase (CBR-CDR) ranges from -19 per 1,000 to +19 per 1,000 (five year rates).

The degree of variation in these rates is dependent on the number of events. Since the artificial populations are growing, the number of births and deaths show a steady rise throughout the runs. For example, the number of births in a five year period varies from 32 during the first years of one run to 275 during the last five years of the fastest-growing run. The tendency for variation to diminish as population size increases is illustrated in Figure 7.4, a graph of the crude rates for one run (which is the median run in terms of variation). Nonetheless, it can be seen that even during the last 50 years of the run when population size exceeds 500 and births and deaths during each period exceed 100, considerable variation persists in the rates. For both rates, this variation exceeds 20 percent of the mean value. It may be recalled that the rule of thumb proposed by Barclay (1958) quoted in chapter 5 was that differences of 10 percent of the mean were to

SIMULATION

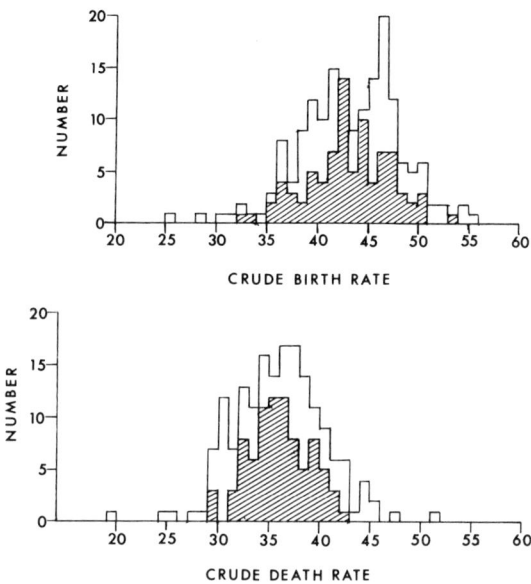

Fig. 7.3 Distribution of crude rates for all runs. The outer histogram represents crude rates calculated on the basis of five-year intervals; the inner, hatched histogram shows rates calculated on ten-year intervals.

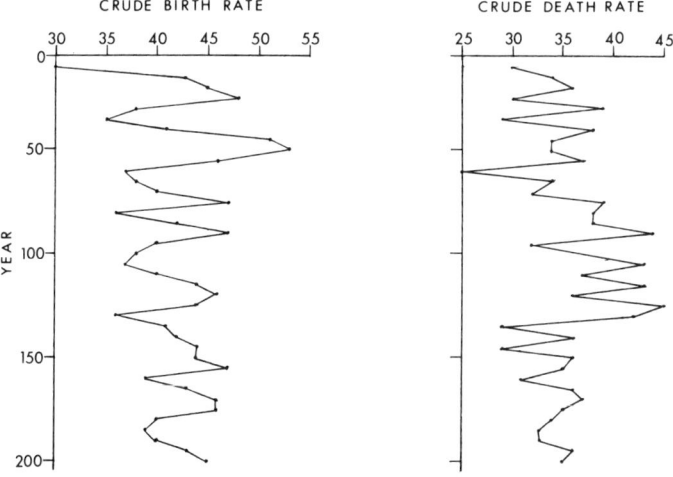

Fig. 7.4 Variation of crude rates through time.

be discounted. Present results suggest at least doubling that value for anthropological populations of 500 or less.

Population growth or extinction has often been used in simulation studies to measure the effect of marriage rules in small populations (Hammel and Hutchinson 1974, Morgan 1974). The experience of these investigators has been that population growth fluctuates widely from run to run. MacCluer et al. (1971) for example, record a range of growth rates from -0.0022 to 0.0045 in fifteen 200 year runs of their simulation of the Yanomama Indian population. With only four runs utilized in the present study, the range may be expected to be less. The fastest-growing population grew at an annual rate of 0.0081; the slowest at 0.0062.

The variation in growth from year to year within each run is perhaps of more interest than these values summed over 200 years of the runs. Certainly for the fieldworker concerned with the estimation of growth rates for his or her small population over a census interval, these values would be relevant. Figure 7.5 presents the distribution of annual growth rates calculated as ten year averages for the four 200 year runs. As was true of the other distributions already discussed, these values are obtained from growing populations. Beginning with 272 individuals, the average final population size was 953. Therefore, the growth rate calculated on the basis of the census interval years 190 to 200 is based on a much larger population than that calculated from growth during the interval years 10 to 20. Several, but not all, of the extreme values showing in the figure were obtained from small populations during the early portions of the runs. One of the highest values, however, occurred as one population grew from 612 to 706 during a 10 year span. When only populations exceeding

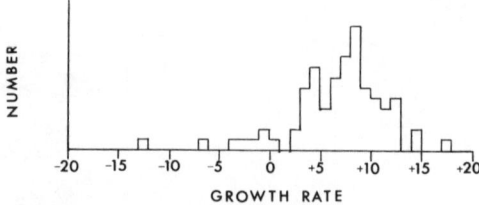

Fig. 7.5 Distribution of annual growth rates based on ten-year intervals for four 200-year runs.

500 individuals are considered, the range from -0.001 to 0.014 is still wide.

These growth values suggest that a considerable degree of fluctuation may occur in populations of at least moderate size (circa 500). Moreover, the artificial populations are essentially closed to migration. In real populations experiencing growth or decline due to a combination of births, deaths and migration, an even greater range might be expected. It is true that in real populations random fluctuations in birth, death, or migration rates are not the only contributors to variation in growth rates but epidemics and accidents (such as those documented for Tristan da Cunha by Roberts 1968) may also occur. Once again, the observed variation in rates is a counsel for caution in interpreting field data.

In order to summarize and further illustrate the results of the simulation work, five populations were chosen randomly from the runs. The averages for ten years preceding the index year were computed. These are presented in Table 7.5. The degree of variation reflects what might be found in a group of five populations of mean size of 500 individuals experiencing the same underlying rates. Alternatively, any one of the populations might be that obtained by chance by a field worker. In fact, the actual variation in field-estimated rates would probably be considerably greater than presented here since migration and other factors would also be operating and errors in the records and/or recall of individuals would undoubtedly occur. The degree of deviation from the underlying rates represented here might be the *best* that the anthropological demographer can expect to encounter.

The importance of the differences between populations in Table 7.5 depends on the interests and purposes of the investigator. To take the case of the field worker attempting to fit a model to data, the concern would be to arrive at an adequate characterization of the demography of the population from scanty data. Depending on the luck of the draw, several different pictures might be obtained. For example, a good fit to the female values in run 3-200 could be obtained from Weiss' (1973) MT: 30-65 with an annual rate of growth of 0.009. In this model population, $_1q_0$ is 0.167, the crude birth rate is about 41 per 1,000, the crude death rate is about 32 per 1,000 and C_{15} is 0.421. These are all quite close to the figures for this run in Table 7.5. It is not, however, the true model population, i.e., the model life table which was used as input in the program Weiss', MT: 30-60. At the same time it

TABLE 7.5
VARIATION IN BASIC DEMOGRAPHIC PARAMETERS FOR FIVE RANDOMLY SELECTED ARTIFICIAL POPULATIONS

Run-Year*	Mid-Period Population	Birth Rate	Death Rate	Infant Death Rate	Growth Rate	C_{15}		c_x-$c_x$stable	
						Male	Female	Male	Female
3-200	818	41.4	32.9	.174	.0086	.380	.429	.113	.151
4-90	542	44.5	41.6	.214	.0029	.364	.383	.219	.165
2-60	341	43.1	38.7	.170	.0042	.350	.455	.164	.173
2-110	418	46.7	36.6	.185	.0098	.372	.444	.171	.119
5-100	473	45.9	37.6	.203	.0082	.430	.400	.156	.155
Stable† Model	—	43.0	35.0	.200	.0070	.379	.412	—	—

*Five ten-year periods were selected from the runs via a random number table (e.g., 3-200 refers to the 200th year of run 3). The rates were calculated as ten year averages; population composition is as of the index year.

†Adjusted for the absence of individuals aged 65 or greater.

is quite close. Adult mortality in both models is the same ($e_{15}=30$) and juvenile mortality is only one step removed from the true value ($l_{15} = 65$ vs. $l_{15} = 60$). For many purposes, this might be felt to be an insignificant difference. Indeed, on the range of models available in the Weiss tables, these are almost identical. Potentially, then, if other factors such as migration and errors of estimation can be controlled, close approximations to the underlying mortality schedule might be obtained even in relatively small populations subject to random fluctuations.

On the other hand, any theoretical application of demography to the problems of anthropology or genetics must either be insensitive to fluctuations or take them into account. No small population will probably ever achieve the stable age distribution; nor will its growth rates cease fluctuating.

Finally, Howell's (1973) statement of what might be an optimum strategy for anthropological demography can be cited. She suggests a combination of empirically-based estimates of parameters, model stable populations, and simulation to explore the demography of technologically primitive populations. The concern of this chapter has been to document variability in small populations. The program developed here may be further applied in a variety of more problem-oriented contexts. The fact of variability may then be translated into the significance of variability.

CHAPTER VIII

CONCLUSIONS

Anthropological demography, like both its parent disciplines, may most fruitfully be used as a comparative approach. The present work has been concerned with the description of one population. Much of the effort has been directed toward achieving a good description from relatively scanty data. Problems such as age misestimation and the consistency of the empirical estimates have loomed large. Although these technical difficulties are present in traditional demography, they are especially weighty in small, non-literate anthropological populations. Using a combination of empirical estimates for the parameters and stable population methods, an internally consistent description of the relatively unacculturated portion of the Semai has been made. In the broad sense, however, this is only an initial step in the process of arriving at valid generalizations about anthropological populations. As other such descriptions become available, hypotheses concerning the impact of demographic features on social organization and/or genetic structure may be refined. General theory concerning demographic processes is not lacking but good data and well-tested specific hypotheses are relatively few.

Howell (1973) has provided a series of statements in the form of hypotheses directed primarily toward hunting and gathering populations. However, they seem generally applicable to any anthropological population. Some are more testable than others but as guidelines they seem useful. In order to summarize and at least minimally compare the Semai work to a more general universe, her hypotheses will be briefly considered below.

Howell's first hypothesis is that technologically primitive populations will not differ in their basic biology from demographically better known populations. Maturation rates and the shapes of the mortality and fertility schedules should lie within the known ranges of these variables. Since the known ranges are quite wide (if one includes historical demography among them) this seems a safe hypothesis. Indeed, it may be necessary to assume that a population is not wildly aberrant in order to apply stable population methods. Certainly the Semai seem normal enough in terms of onset of childbearing and shapes of the fertility and mortality schedules. The age-specific fertility curve is almost the same as the mean values found by Weiss (1973) in his study of anthropological populations and is similar to the general world pattern which is low in the 15-19 age bracket, rises to maximum at 25-29, and tapers to zero at age 45 (see chapter 6). Likewise, the age-specific mortality curve based on the empirical data showed a good fit to Weiss' model life tables. Again, the general pattern of death by age for the Semai fits that to be expected in better known human populations.

The difficulties of disproving this hypothesis should be noted. The lack of high quality data and the small size of most anthropological populations make acceptable counter-cases almost impossible to produce. As may be seen in chapter 7, random differences from the underlying true rates from year to year and decade to decade may be quite large. The fieldworker may well find a situation beyond previously recorded experience; the most likely outcome of such a finding, however, will be rejection of the data unless the case is much better documented than is usually true in anthropological demography. In most cases, this rejection will probably be justified. To illustrate: based on field collected data, I hypothesized (Fix 1971) that the high overall Semai sex ratio might be due to a higher than normal sex ratio at birth, (i.e., greater than 1.07). Even though the sample size was small, the null hypothesis of sex ratio at birth equal to 1.07 could be rejected at the .05 level. Now, after examination of the larger census from the whole East Semai population and the fitting of male and female life tables, the much simpler hypothesis of differential mortality between the sexes has been established (see chapter 6). In this case, chance factors (more male births) and perhaps a tendency for women to report dead offspring as males more often than actually occurred, biased the data.

Thus, although stated as an hypothesis, Howell's first point may perhaps better be considered as an assumption or heuristic. Assume that anthropological populations are similar in basic

CONCLUSIONS

pattern to other known human populations and distrust any result which suggests otherwise. Only very strong evidence might be accepted which is counter to the general experience.

Several of Howell's hypotheses may be condensed into the statement that people have little ability to influence mortality rates and some ability to control fertility and migration; therefore, mortality will be the controlling variable to which fertility and migration rates are adjusted. Few data relevant to this point have been considered in this study. Now, as medical care is becoming a real option for the East Semai, the choice of life or death may be possible. It was also suggested (see chapter 5), that infanticide by neglect may be a factor in raising the Semai infant death rate. However, Howell's general statement seems to fit the Semai situation reasonably well. The principal cause of death (chapter 5) is disease. Although populations may vary with respect to the effect that their cultural practices may have on the incidence of infectious diseases (e.g., Alland 1970), it seems fair to say that Semai efforts to cure organic disease are relatively ineffectual. Since their conception of disease is supernatural (Dentan 1968), conscious effective devices to prevent diseases are not carried out. Some few customs may limit the spread of disease, such as that which dictates that water wherever possible should be collected from small streams descending from the hills rather than from the main stream which is the place of defecation, and the relatively dispersed settlement pattern of unacculturated Semai probably limits the spread of some diseases. On the other hand, customary Semai food-sharing patterns may cause disease-sharing, just as the communal "sings" held to cure sick individuals may spread the disease. Clearly, the detailed exploration of this hypothesis would involve considerable further work.

In a similar manner, a variety of Semai customs may affect fertility. Conscious fertility control is not characteristic of the Semai. Semai ideology places value on children although the pressure seems less than in some other societies. Almost all women are married by age of fifteen and most stay married throughout their reproductive lives. Even with relatively high mortality rates, widows are able to remarry quickly and lose little time at risk to childbearing. Divorce in the early years of marriage is common; if women are physiologically sterile, they are unlikely to remain married, or if the husband is responsible, the woman is soon married to a fertile spouse. The excess female mortality resulting in a high sex ratio insures that all women may potentially find a mate.

Still, a number of factors (discussed in chapters 3 and 5) serve to limit family size. Perhaps the most important is the relatively long space between births, an average of one live-birth per five years per woman throughout the reproductive span (see chapter 6). The actual mechanism responsible for this spacing is not known although it was speculated that nutritional factors in combination with an extended nursing period might play a role (after Frisch and McArthur 1974). Post-partum sex taboos do not seem to be significant and abortion is not practiced.

A further specification of levels of mortality and fertility and their consequences for population limitation or growth has been made by Howell. She hypothesizes that mortality in primitive populations will vary from the highest level which can be balanced by biologically attainable fertility levels (e_0=18-20 years) to more moderate levels (e_0=35 to 40 years) and that fertility will range from high to moderate (completed family sizes from ten to five offspring). The Semai fall within this range showing both moderate mortality (male e_0=31.3; female, 28.3) and moderate total fertility (completed fertility of 5.73 offspring). Tying in with this moderate level of mortality, population growth should be higher in the Semai than in populations subject to more rigorous conditions. While not high by the standards of many developing countries (some reach growth rates of 3 percent per annum), the best estimate of the East Semai growth rate would lead to substantial growth in the long run ($r=0.7$ percent).

Migration, according to Howell, will serve as an adjustment mechanism for segments of populations experiencing local growth. The calculated frequency of migration will depend on the units chosen for analysis. But at the settlement level at least, Semai migration rates are very high (see chapter 5). Over the long run, the total Semai population may be conceptualized as a series of clusters which break up and reform with continual exchange between them. One factor in this continued rearrangement may be local population growth. The results of this computer simulation (chapter 7) suggest that rather large differences in growth rates may occur between local groups. On the other side of the coin, it is probably true that very small settlements would not survive without substantial in-migration (Fix 1973). In any case, the lack of serious barriers to local migration among the Semai allows migration to serve in the manner indicated by Howell. That the decision to migrate by individuals or the actual frequency of migration is determined by local population pressure is a more complicated question (see Fix 1975).

The final hypothesis proposed by Howell relates to the possibility of identifying types of hunting and gathering societies based on their underlying demographic structures. That is, she suggests that other cultural domains will respond to basic demographic constraints, and societies differing in history and geography will nonetheless show basic similarities in a variety of cultural features. The answer to this question must await the collection of further comparative material. If it is true that socio-cultural characteristics depend directly on demographic parameters, then it follows logically that what Howell says is true. Given the complexity of cultural causation, even the most optimistic anthropological demographer may not expect cultural identity between demographically similar populations. What one may reasonably hope for is similarity in certain kinds of socio-cultural items. One obvious feature of social organization, marriage patterns, may be expected to be strongly influenced by demographic parameters and thus show similarities between different cultures. For example, populations such as the Semai having a skewed sex ratio in favor of males might be expected to show a similar pattern of wide age differences between spouses (see chapter 3).

The Semai case suggests that Howell's restriction of her hypothesis to hunters and gatherers may well be too limiting for fruitful comparison. In terms of their demographic structures, hunters and gatherers may not be easily separated from some populations of swiddeners. As a case in point, Howell (1974) fit the !Kung Bushman population with a West Model Table at level 5 (Coale and Demeny 1966). Interestingly, this model life table is quite similar to the Weiss model fit to the Semai data (!Kung e_0 male is 27.7, female, is 30.0. Semai e_0 male is 31.3, female is 28.3). According to Howell, therefore, there should exist broad similarities between !Kung and Semai in social organization and culture.

I would agree with Howell that for many purposes hunters and gatherers do not form a single category of analysis. I would extend her argument to say that neither is "horticulturalists" a uniform category. The larger point to make is that hunters and gatherers may not be the only useful reference group for inferring the population structure of earlier human populations. It is almost certain that early hominids were hunters and gatherers. But it does not follow that all features of their organization would correspond to the modern societies practicing this technology. Indeed, the hunters and gatherers of the Northwest Coast of North America were possibly as sedentary as the Semai. This may have been equally true of past populations as well. Perhaps the best strategy would be to treat demographic factors as variables to be examined in relation to environment and social organization rather than to construct typologies of hunter/gatherers or horticulturalists. In this way, data from a variety of extant anthropological populations may be employed to reconstruct past populations through the understanding of the relationship between fertility and mortality levels, migration, environment and culture.

BIBLIOGRAPHY

Alland, A.
    1970   Adaptation in cultural evolution: an approach to medical anthropology. New York: Columbia University Press.

Baharon, Azar bin Raffie'i
    1967   The New World of the Orang Asli. Mimeographed. Kuala Lumpur: Department of Aboriginal Affairs.

Barclay, G.W.
    1958   Techniques of population analysis. New York: John Wiley.

Beals, A.R., G. Splinder, and L. Spindler
    1973   Culture in process. New York: Holt, Rinehart and Winston.

Benjamin, G.
    1966a   Temiar phonology and morphology: an outline. Unpublished manuscript. Kings College, Cambridge.
    1966b   Temiar Social Groupings. Federation Museums Journal 11:1-75.
    1973   Introduction. Among the forest dwarfs of Malaya, second impression. Kuala Lumpur: Oxford University Press.

Birdsell, J.B.
    1957   Some population problems involving Pleistocene man. Cold Spring Harbor Symposia in Quantitative Biology 22: 47-69.
    1968   Some predictions of the Pleistocene based on equilibrium systems among recent hunter-gatherers. *In:* Man the hunter, edited by R. B. Lee and I. Devore. Chicago: Aldine.

Bolton, J.M.
    1968   Medical services to the aborigines in West Malaya. British Medical Journal 2:818-23.

Boyce, A.J., C.F. Kuchemann, and G.A. Harrison
    1967   Neighbourhood knowledge and the distribution of marriage distances. Annals of Human Genetics 30:335-38.

Brass, W., A.J. Coale, P. Demeny, D.F. Heisel, F. Lorimer, A. Romaniuk, and E. Van de Walle
    1968   The demography of tropical Africa. Princeton: Princeton University Press.

Cant, R.C.
    1972   An historical geography of Pahang. Monographs of the Malaysian Branch Royal Asiatic Society No. 4. Singapore.

Carey, I.
　1973　The administration of the aboriginal tribes of western Malaysia. IXth International Congress of Anthropological and Ethnological Sciences, Chicago.

Carneiro, R.L.
　1960　Slash and burn agriculture: a closer look at its implications for settlement patterns. Man and culture. Selected papers of the 5th International Congress of Anthropological and Ethnological Sciences, edited by A.F.C. Wallace. Philadelphia: University of Pennsylvania Press.

Carr-Saunders, A.M.
　1922　The population problem: a study of human evolution. Oxford: Clarendon Press.

Cavalli-Sforza, L.L. and W.F. Bodmer
　1971　The genetics of human populations. San Francisco: W.H. Freeman.

Coale, A.J. and P. Demeny
　1966　Regional model life tables and stable populations. Princeton: Princeton University Press.

Dentan, R.K.
　1964　Senoi. *In:* Ethnic groups of mainland Southeast Asia, edited by F.M. Lebar, G.C. Hickey and J.K. Musgrave. New Haven: Human Relations Area Files Press.
　1965　Some Senoi Semai dietary restrictions: a study of food behavior in a Malayan Hill Tribe. Unpublished doctoral dissertation, Yale University.
　1968　The Semai: a nonviolent people of Malaya. New York: Holt, Rinehart and Winston.
　1971　Some Senoi Semai planting techniques. Economic Botany 25:136-59.

Diffloth, G.F.
　1968　Proto-Semai phonology. Federation Museums Journal 13:65-74.

Dubos, R.
　1965　Mankind adapting. New Haven: Yale University Press.

Dunn, F.L.
　1966　Radiocarbon dating of the Malayan Neolithic. Proceedings of the Prehistoric Society 23:352-53.
　1970　Cultural evolution in the Late Pleistocene and Holocene of Southeast Asia. American Anthropologist 72:1041-53.

Dyke, B. and J.W. MacCluer
　1973　Estimation of vital rates by means of Monte Carlo simulation. Demography 10:383-403.
　1974　Computer simulation in human population studies. New York: Academic Press.

Fix, A.G.
　1971　Semai Senoi population structure and genetic microdifferentiation. Unpublished doctoral dissertation. University of Michigan.
　1973　Potential mate pools, endogamy, and local breeding populations of Semai Senoi. Read at the annual meeting of the American Anthropological Association, New Orleans, Louisiana.

1974   Neighbourhood knowledge and marriage distance: the Semai case. Annals of Human Genetics 37:327-32.

1975   Fission-fusion and lineal effect: aspects of the population structure of Semai Senoi of Malaysia. American Journal of Physical Anthropology 43:295-302.

Fix, A.G. and Luan Eng Lie-Injo
1975   Genetic microdifferentiation in the Semai Senoi of Malaysia. American Journal of Physical Anthropology 43:47-55.

Frisch, R.E. and J.W. McArthur
1974   Menstrual cycles: fatness as a determinant of miminum weight for height necessary for their maintenance or onset. Science 185:949-51.

Hajnal, J.
1963   Concepts of random mating and the frequency of consanguineous marriages. Proceedings of the Royal Society 159:125-77.

Hammel, E.A. and D. Hutchinson
1974   Two tests of computer microsimulation: the effect of an incest tabu on population viability, and the effect of age differences between spouses on the skewing of consanguineal relationships between them. *In*: Computer simulation in human population studies. B. Dyke and J. MacCluer, eds. New York: Academic Press.

Howell, N.
1973   The feasibility of demographic studies in "Anthropological" populations. *In*: Methods and theories of anthropological genetics, edited by M.H. Crawford and P.L. Workman. Albuquerque: University of New Mexico Press.

1974   An empirical perspective on simulation models of human population. *In*: Computer simulation in human population studies, edited by B. Dyke and J.W. MacCluer. New York: Academic Press.

Jain, K.K., T.C. Hsu, R. Freedman, and M.C. Chang
1970   Demographic aspects of lactation and postpartum amenorrhea. Demography 7:255-71.

Kennedy, J.
1967   A history of Malaya. London: Macmillan.

Keyfitz, N.
1969   Introduction to the mathematics of population. Reading: Addison-Wesley.

Keyfitz, N. and W. Flieger
1971   Population: facts and methods of demography. San Francisco: W.H. Freeman.

Krzywicki, L.
1934   Primitive society and its vital statistics. London: Macmillan.

Lebar, F.M., G.C. Hickey and J.K. Musgrave, Editors.
1964   Ethnic groups of mainland Southeast Asia. New Haven: Human Relations Area Files Press.

Lorimer, F., M. Fortes, K. A. Busia, A. I. Richards, P. Reining, and G. Mortara.
1954   Culture and human fertility. Paris: UNESCO.

MacCluer, J.W.
  1973 Computer simulation in anthropology and human genetics. *In*: Methods and theories of anthropological genetics, edited by M.H. Crawford and P.L. Workman. Albuquerque: University of New Mexico Press.

MacCluer, J.W., J.V. Neel and N.A. Chagnon
  1971 Demographic structure of a primitive population: a simulation. American Journal of Physical Anthropology 35:193-207.

Montagu M.F.A.
  1957 The reproductive development of the female. New York: Julian Press.

Morgan, K.
  1974 Computer simulation of incest prohibition and clan proscription rules in closed finite populations. *In*: Computer simulation in human population studies, edited by B. Dyke and J. MacCluer. New York: Academic Press.

Nag, Moni
  1962 Factors affecting human fertility in non-industrial societies: a cross-cultural study. Yale University Publications in Anthropology, No. 66.

Neel, J.V.
  1970 Lessons from a primitive people. Science 170:815-22.

Neel, J.V. and N. Chagnon
  1968 The demography of two tribes of primitive relatively unacculturated American Indians. Proceedings of the National Academy of Sciences 59:680-89.

Neel J.V., F.M. Salzano, P.C. Junqueira, F. Keiter and D. Maybury-Lewis
  1964 Studies on the Xavante Indians of the Brazilian Mato Grosso. American Journal of Human Genetics 16:52-140.

Neel, J.V. and F.M. Salzano
  1964 A prospectus for genetic studies of the American Indian. Cold Spring Harbor Symposium in Quantitative Biology 29:85-98.
  1967 Further studies on the Xavante Indians X. Some hypotheses-generalizations resulting from these studies. American Journal of Human Genetics 19:554-74.

Neel, J.V. and K.M. Weiss
  1975 The genetic structure of a tribal population, the Yanomama Indians. American Journal of Physical Anthropology 42:25-51.

Noone, H.D.
  1939 Some vital statistics of the Lowland Senoi of Perak. Journal of the Federated Malay States Museums 15:195-215.

Pearce, J.
  1944 Malay language. Singapore: Malaya Publishing House.

Polunin, I.
  1953 The medical natural history of Malayan Aborigines. Medical Journal of Malaya 8:62-174.

Roberts, D.F.
  1968 Genetic effects of population size reduction. Nature 220:1084-88.

Salzano, F.M., J.V. Neel and D. Maybury-Lewis
    1967   Further studies on the Xavante Indians. I. Demographic data on two additional villages: genetic structure of the tribe. American Journal of Human Genetics 19:463-89.

Tufo, M.V. del
    1949   Malaya, comprising the federation of Malaya and the colony of Singapore: a report on the 1947 census of population. London.

United Nations
    1967   Methods of estimating basic demographic measures from incomplete data. Manuals on Methods of Estimating Population, Manual IV. New York: United Nations.

Visaria, P.M.
    1963   The sex ratio of the population of India. Unpublished doctoral dissertation. Princeton: Princeton University Press.
    1967   Sex ratio at birth in territories with a relatively complete registration. Eugenics Quarterly 14:132-42.

Weiss, K.M.
    1973   Demographic models for anthropology. Memoirs of the Society for American Archaeology, No. 27.

Wilkinson, R.J.
    1932   A Malay-English dictionary. Mykilene, Greece: Salavopoulos and Kinderlis.

Williams-Hunt, P.D.R.
    1952   An introduction to the Malayan aborigines. Kuala Lumpur: Government Press.

20. The Accokeek Creek Site: A Middle Atlantic Seaboard Culture Sequence, by Robert L. Stephenson and Alice L. Ferguson with selections by Henry G. Ferguson. 1963. Pages 251, 30 figures, 18 plates, Price $3.00.
21. The Steuben Village and Mounds: A Multicomponent Late Hopewell Site in Illinois, by Dan F. Morse. 1963. Pages 134, 6 figures, 31 plates. Price $2.50.
22. Bibliography of Michigan Archaeology, by Alexis A. Praus. 1964. Pages 77. Price $2.00.
23. Aboriginal Relationships Between Culture and Plant Life in the Upper Great Lakes Region, by Richard Asa Yarnell. 1964. Pages 218, 1 figure, 4 maps. Price $2.50.
24. Late Woodland Cultures of Southeastern Michigan, by James E. Fitting. 1965. Pages 165, 20 figures, 48 plates. Price $3.00.
25. Studies in the Natural Radioactivity of Prehistoric Materials, edited by Arthur J. Jelinek and James E. Fitting. 1965. Pages 97, 2 charts, 10 figures. Price $2.00.
26. Two Stratified Sites on the Door Peninsula of Wisconsin, by Ronald J. Mason, 1966. Pages 261, 10 figures, 24 plates. Price $3.00.
27. The Paleo-Indian Occupation of Holcombe Beach, by James E. Fitting, Jerry DeVisscher, and Edward J. Wahla. 1966. Pages 160, 20 figures, 12 plates. Price $2.50.
28. The Fort Ancient Aspect, by James B. Griffin. 1966, reissue of 1943 edition. Pages 734, 18 figures, 10 maps, 157 plates. Price $6.00.
29. The Prehistoric Animal Ecology and Ethnozoology of the Upper Great Lakes Region, by Charles E. Cleland. 1966. Pages 294, 5 figures, 40 tables, 23 maps. Price $3.00.
30. The Juntunen Site and the Late Woodland Prehistory of the Upper Great Lakes Area, by Alan L. McPherron. 1967. Pages 316, 43 figures, 30 tables, 57 plates. Price $4.00.
31. A Prehistoric Sequence in the Middle Pecos Valley, New Mexico, by Arthur J. Jelinek. 1967. Pages 190, 21 figures, 16 plates. Price $3.00.
32. Contributions to Michigan Archaeology, by James E. Fitting. John R. Halsey, and H. Martin Wobst. 1968. Pages 275, 19 figures, 42 plates. Price $3.00.
33. Ohio Hopewell Ceramics: An Analysis of the Extant Collections, by Olaf H. Prufer. 1968. Pages 156, 29 figures, 16 plates. Price $3.00.
34. The Prehistory of the Burnt Bluff Area, assembled by James E. Fitting. 1968. Pages 140, 47 figures. Price $3.00.
35. The Lithic Industries of the Illinois Valley in the Early and Middle Woodland Period, by Anta Montet-White. 1968. Pages 200, 65 figures. Price $3.00.
36. The Naomikong Point Site and the Dimensions of Laurel in the Lake Superior Region, by Donald E. Janzen. 1968. Pages 152, 12 figures, 21 plates. Price $3.00.
37. Obsidian Analyses and Prehistoric Near Eastern Trade: 7500 to 3500 B.C., by Gary A. Wright. 1969. Pages 92, 11 tables, 7 figures. Price $2.00.
38. The Administration of Rural Production in an Early Mesopotamian Town, by Henry T. Wright, contributions by Sandor Bokonyi, Kent V. Flannery, and John Mayhall. 1969. Pages 162, 29 figures, 15 tables. Price $3.00.
39. Rules of Descent: Studies in the Sociology of Parentage, by Guy E. Swanson. 1969. Pages 108, 4 figures, 7 tables. Price $2.00.
40. Early Puebloan Occupations at Tesuque By-Pass and the Upper Rio Grande Valley, by Charles H. McNutt. 1969. Pages 140, 13 figures, 11 plates. Price $3.00.
41. The Archaeology of Summer Island: Changing Settlement Systems in Northern Lake Michigan, by David S. Brose. 1970. Pages 236, 31 tables, 17 figures, 35 plates. Price $3.00.
42. The Occupations of Migrants in Ghana, by Polly Hill. 1970. Pages 84, 11 tables. Price $2.00.
43. Prehistoric Biological Relationships in the Great Lakes Region, by Richard Guy Wilkinson. 1971. Pages 168, 40 tables, 33 figures, 2 plates. Price $3.50.
44. Property Control and Social Strategies: Settlers on a Middle Eastern Plain, by Barbara C. Aswad. 1971. Pages 180, 16 tables, 16 figures, 17 plates, 12 appendixes. Price $4.00.
45. Miscellaneous Studies in Mexican Prehistory, by Michael W. Spence, Jeffrey R. Parsons, and Mary Hrones Parsons. 1972. Pages 170, 24 figures, 54 plates, 4 maps. Price $4.00.
46. Social Exchange and Interaction, edited by Edwin N. Wilmsen. 1972. Pages 147, 10 figures, 7 tables. Price $3.00.
47. The Prehistoric People of the Fort Ancient Culture of the Central Ohio Valley, by Louise M. Robbins and Georg K. Neumann. 1972. Pages 713, 2 figures, 285 tables, 54 plates. Price $6.00.